For Marlina Alba

PETER ZUMTHOR
2008–2013

Buildings and Projects
Volume 5

Edited by Thomas Durisch

Scheidegger & Spiess

Volume 1   1985–1989

What I Do

Atelier Zumthor, Haldenstein, Graubünden
Shelter for Roman Archaeological Ruins, Chur, Graubünden
Caplutta Sogn Benedetg, Sumvitg, Graubünden
Spittelhof Housing Complex, Biel-Benken near Basel
Rindermarkt Apartment Building, Zurich
Rothorn Gondola Station, Valbella, Graubünden
Apartments for Senior Citizens, Masans, Chur, Graubünden
Bregenz Art Museum, Austria

Volume 2   1990–1997

Gugalun House, Versam, Graubünden
Therme Vals, Graubünden
Topography of Terror, Berlin, Germany
Herz Jesu Church, Munich, Germany
Laban Centre for Movement and Dance, London, England
Swiss Sound Box, Expo 2000, Hanover, Germany
Luzi House, Jenaz, Graubünden
Kolumba Art Museum, Cologne, Germany

Volume 3   1998–2001

Poetic Landscape, Bad Salzuflen, Germany
Zumthor House, Haldenstein, Graubünden
Mountain Hotel, Tschlin, Graubünden
I Ching Gallery, Dia Center for the Arts, Beacon, New York, USA
Harjunkulma Apartment Building, Jyväskylä, Finland
Pingus Winery, Valbuena de Duero, Spain
Bruder Klaus Field Chapel, Wachendorf, Germany
Additional Cabins, Pension Briol, Barbian-Dreikirchen, Italy

Volume 4   2002–2007

Galerie Bastian, Berlin, Germany
Redevelopment of De Meelfabriek, Leiden, Holland
Summer Restaurant Insel Ufnau, Lake Zurich
Corporate Learning Center, Aabach Estate, Risch, Zug
Almannajuvet Zinc Mine Museum, Sauda, Norway
Güterareal Residential Development, Lucerne
A Tower for Therme Vals, Graubünden
Leis Houses, Oberhus and Unterhus, Vals, Graubünden
Hisham's Palace, Jericho, Palestinian Territories
Steilneset Memorial, Vardø, Norway

Volume 5   2008–2013

Nomads of Atacama Hotel, San Pedro de Atacama, Chile	7
Bregenzerwald House of Craftsmanship, Andelsbuch, Austria	25
Chivelstone House, Devon, England	43
Los Angeles County Museum of Art, LACMA, California, USA	61
New City Gate with Theater and Café, Isny im Allgäu, Germany	79
Adaptable Theater for Riom Castle, Riom, Graubünden	95
House of Seven Gardens, Doha, Qatar	107
Serpentine Gallery Pavilion, London, England	123
Perm State Art Gallery, Perm, Russia	139
List of Works 1968–2013	155
Texts by Peter Zumthor	168
Biography	170
Collaborators 1985–2013	171
The Work of Many	172
Acknowledgments	174
Picture Credits	176

Nomads of Atacama Hotel, San Pedro de Atacama, Chile
2008 – 2010

My client had acquired a tract of land in the Atacama Desert of Chile near San Pedro de Atacama and invited me to take a look at it. The scale of the landscape captivated me. Everything is big and looks big; everything is far-reaching and far away. The extinct Licancabur volcano dominates the silhouette of the Andes mountain range in the background. The sparse vegetation, scrubby trees, and isolated tufts of grass hardly encourage travelers to linger: one can see that the desert is at the mercy of the wind, driving the sand before it.

But these desert parcels of land, known as *melgas*, have water rights. Water flows down into the desert from the distant Andes in little channels, where it is directed periodically into square retaining pools enclosed within dirt walls. The moment the water flows into the pools, the desert starts turning green. The plant seeds in the sand of the *melgas* have just been waiting for the water.

As an architect whose everyday challenge involves dealing with the valley gorges of the Alpine landscape and responding to densely built and tightly structured situations, in Switzerland and elsewhere, it was a great joy to design something for the desert, for its expanses and wide horizon. Forty-eight hotel rooms laid out on an endless horizon of 360 degrees for people wanting to experience the extremes of nature—this is the design that came out of that joy.

The center of the hotel is an oasis, created with the water that flows into our tract of land every twenty-five days. We use this water to create the special vegetation of an oasis and we store it in basins under the great shell roofs of the hotel, where it provides natural cooling through evaporation.

Structurally, the hotel consists of a ring-shaped roof plate and a shell-like floor plate, which vaults up and down four times, here touching the ground and there melding into the roof plate. The engineers Sven Plieninger and Stefan Justiz from Stuttgart helped us develop the load-bearing structure. Four honeycomb units with lateral cantilevers are combined to make the whole form a ring. The public spaces of the hotel—lobby, restaurant, pool, and the main lounge—are situated in the areas where the floor plate vaults upward.

In these areas, protected by the vaulting roof, we imagine guests spending time out in the open. Supplied with special clothing and blankets, they experience the desert, the winds, and the cold nights, using furniture designed especially for the outdoors. And they warm themselves at open fires, as we had done in San Pedro de Atacama.

Swaying pedestrian bridges lead from the oasis, a large protected courtyard, to the hotel rooms that open out into the landscape. Once in their rooms, the guests live in the view, as if they were on a large windowsill. Beds and bathrooms are in the rear. From there, every room has a stairway up to the roof. The hotel lies 2500 meters above sea level: the night sky is clear, the view of the stars overhead stupendous. I would have enjoyed being there for the hotel's inauguration; I would have taken some woolen blankets, climbed the stairs to the roof, and gazed up into the heavens.

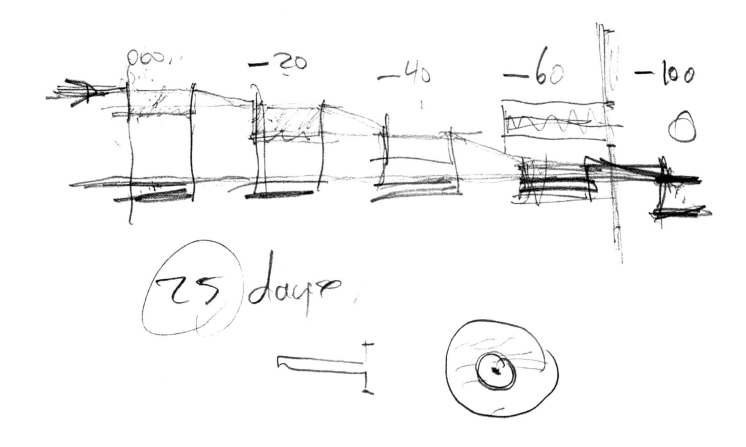

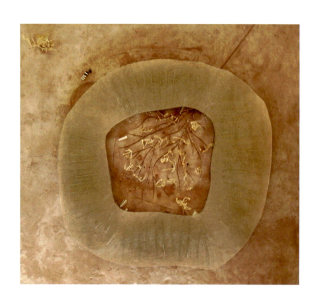

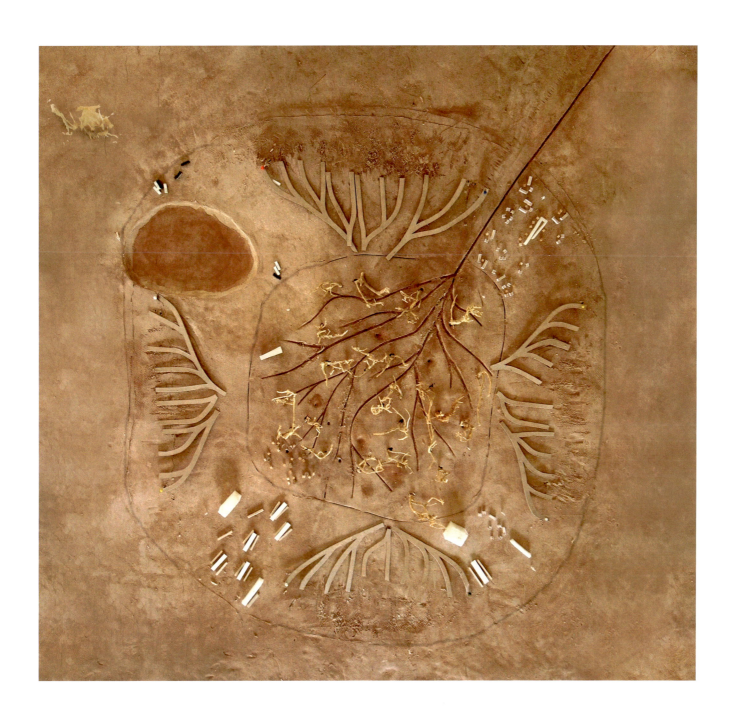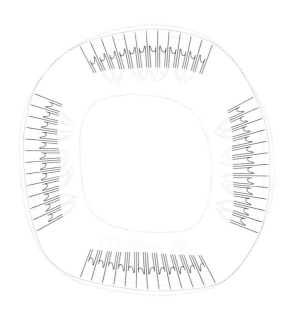

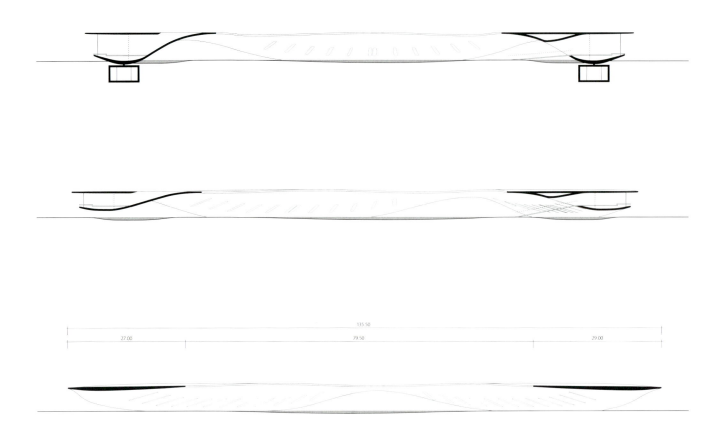

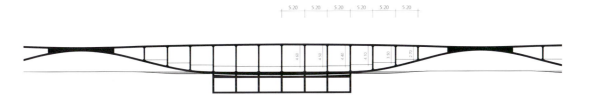

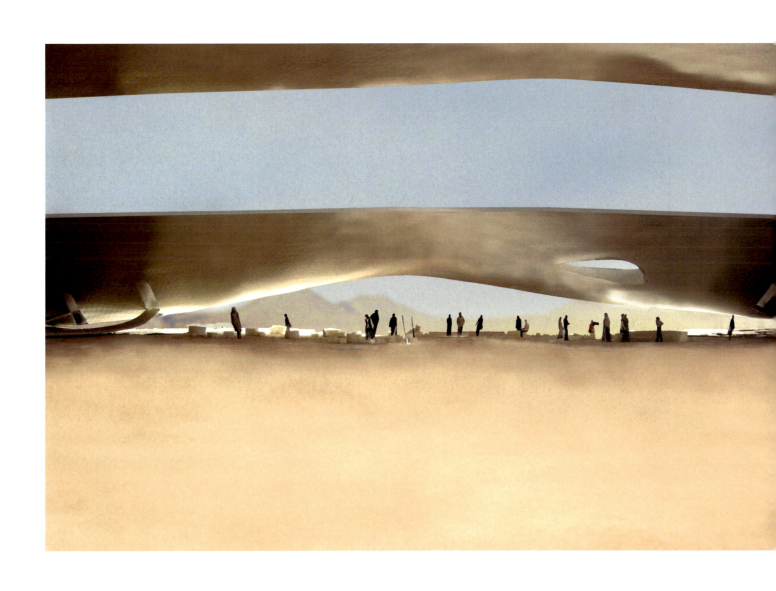

Bregenzerwald House of Craftsmanship, Andelsbuch, Austria
2008–2013

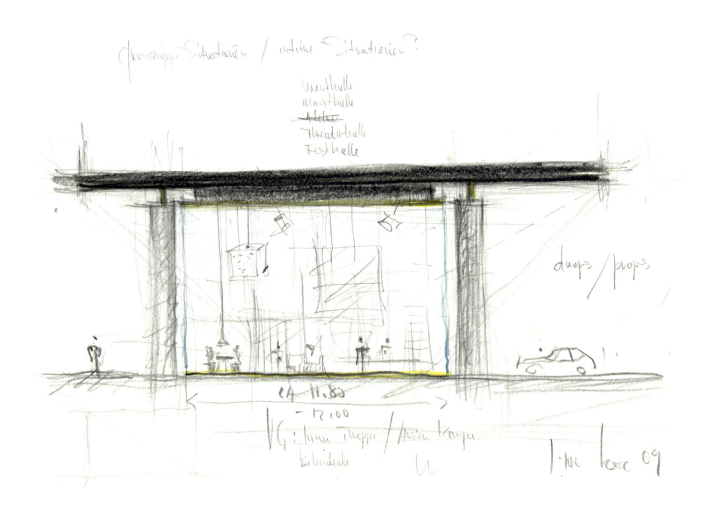

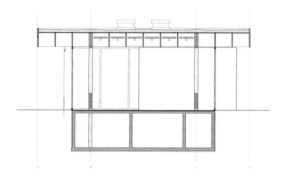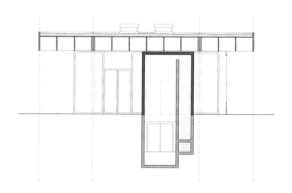

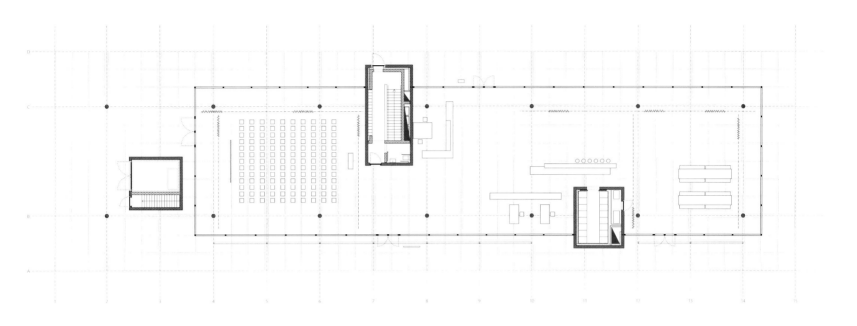
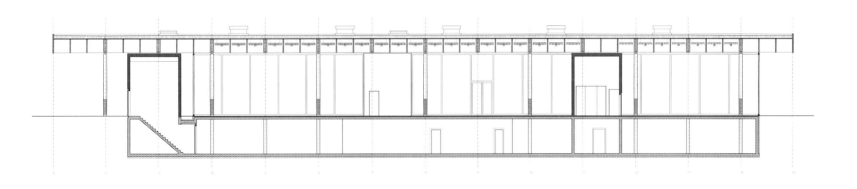

The "werkraum bregenzerwald" is an affiliation founded in 1999 of cabinetmakers, carpenters, builders, plumbers, metalworkers, graphic artists, goldsmiths, upholsterers, and stove-makers. The local artisans wanted to build a craft and design center in their valley, the Bregenzerwald, where they could get together and show their craftsmanship to the public, undertake common projects, make furniture collections and material archives available, hold conversations with clients, schedule seminars and workshops, and celebrate special occasions like the Artisans' Ball with the valley residents.

There was no prototype for this kind of building. So we designed a large glass showcase encompassing 800 square meters of floor space underneath a roof of almost 1,600 square meters with spacious overhangs that cover a good deal of the open area at the old train station in the village of Andelsbuch. Here there is ample space for open-air events, exhibitions, and parties, as well as a parking lot for visitors.

The dark roof that offers shelter for these gatherings is made of wood. As in a factory or a small theater, the technical equipment, providing maximum flexibility for any number of changing situations, is set inside the deep coffers of the roof's frame: background lighting, accent lighting, emergency lighting; electrical connections such as bus bars and sockets; smoke detectors, fire alarms, alarm systems, exit signs, ventilation equipment, smoke extraction systems; and finally, curtains and large dark-blue felt padding to ensure good acoustics.

The roof sits on fourteen thin wooden columns, so-called pendulum supports that are not fix mounted onto the floor or into the ceiling. They need only support the weight of the roof, as it is laterally stabilized by three large hollow concrete blocks. These structures contain auxiliary spaces for elevator, stairwell, and kitchen, and they section the floor plan of the large glass box into three areas that flow into one another.

The building has a commercial character, but is delicately and carefully wrought so that it fits well with the various artisanal enterprises and their high-level work with wood, metal, leather, fabric, paper, glass, or concrete. The artisans of the "werkraum bregenzerwald" are the kind of specialists that we architects are always looking for. It was a pleasure working with them. The Bregenzerwald House of Craftsmanship is a focal point for executing and presenting their accomplishments.

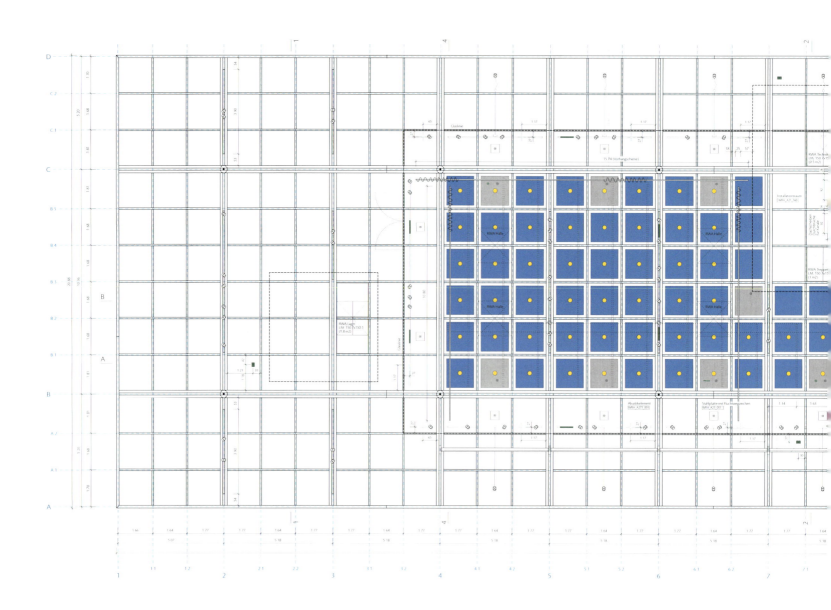

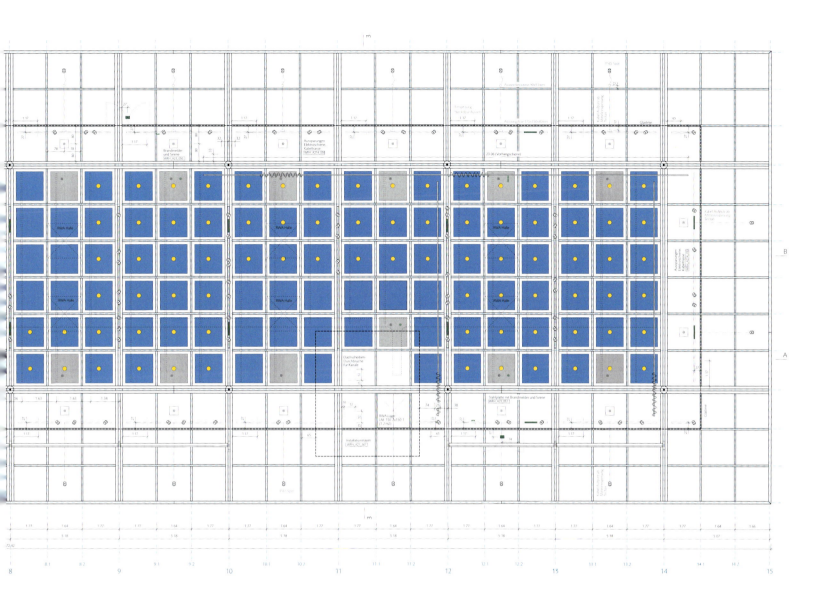

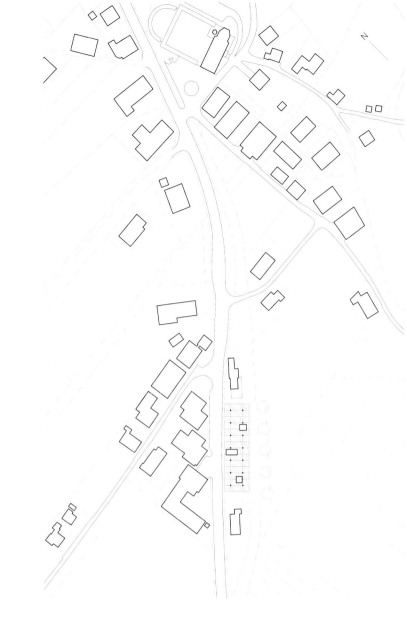

Chivelstone House, Devon, England
since 2008

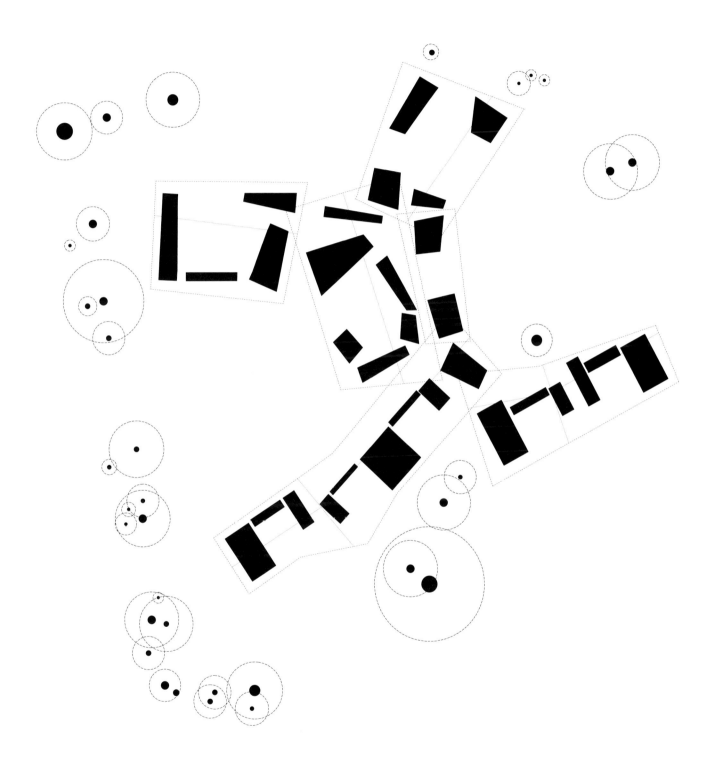

Chivelstone House was conceived as a short-term retreat for small groups of people to vacation, rest, study, or work. It consists of two blocks of bedrooms and a large roof. Its basic materials are the materials and colors of the region: stone, compressed concrete, and wood. Large windows frame the landscape in the bedrooms. The living area is under the large roof plate. It is glazed all around and the landscape flows right through it. The powerful piers supporting the roof stand freely in the room, and in combination with the freestanding cabinet units they give it an open-plan layout. There are areas for cooking, eating, a fireplace, a library, niches with two easy chairs where one can read a book, and even nooks near the kitchen where children can play while their parents are preparing meals.

The house, which our client is building to replace a residence from the 1940s, sits on a hill above the hamlet of Chivelstone. It is surrounded by a circle of old Monterey pines, which were planted around the former house: a gift from America, the locals say. The view of the green Devon landscape with its gently rolling hills has a calming effect. The sea is nearby. The Atlantic coast is less than an hour's walk away. The only reminders now of the old house, besides the Monterey pines, are traces of site modifications, small stone retaining walls built with the local technique known as "shillet on edge," and a hexagonal flower bed with a concrete surround, said to have been constructed by the former mistress of the house.

The spot on the hill has a cheerful serenity that seems to derive from its history.

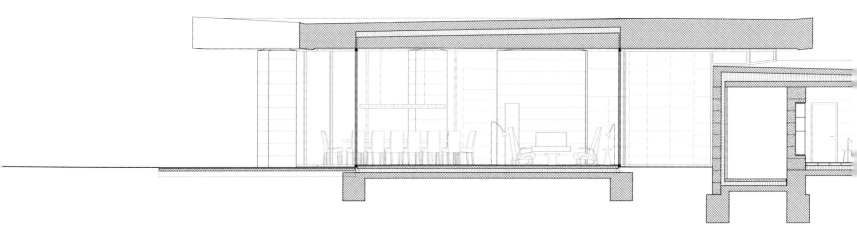

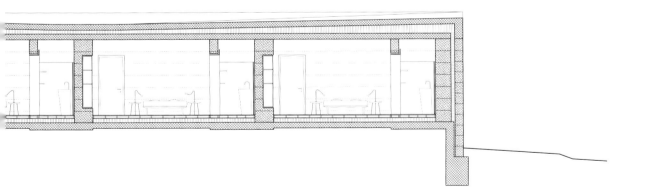

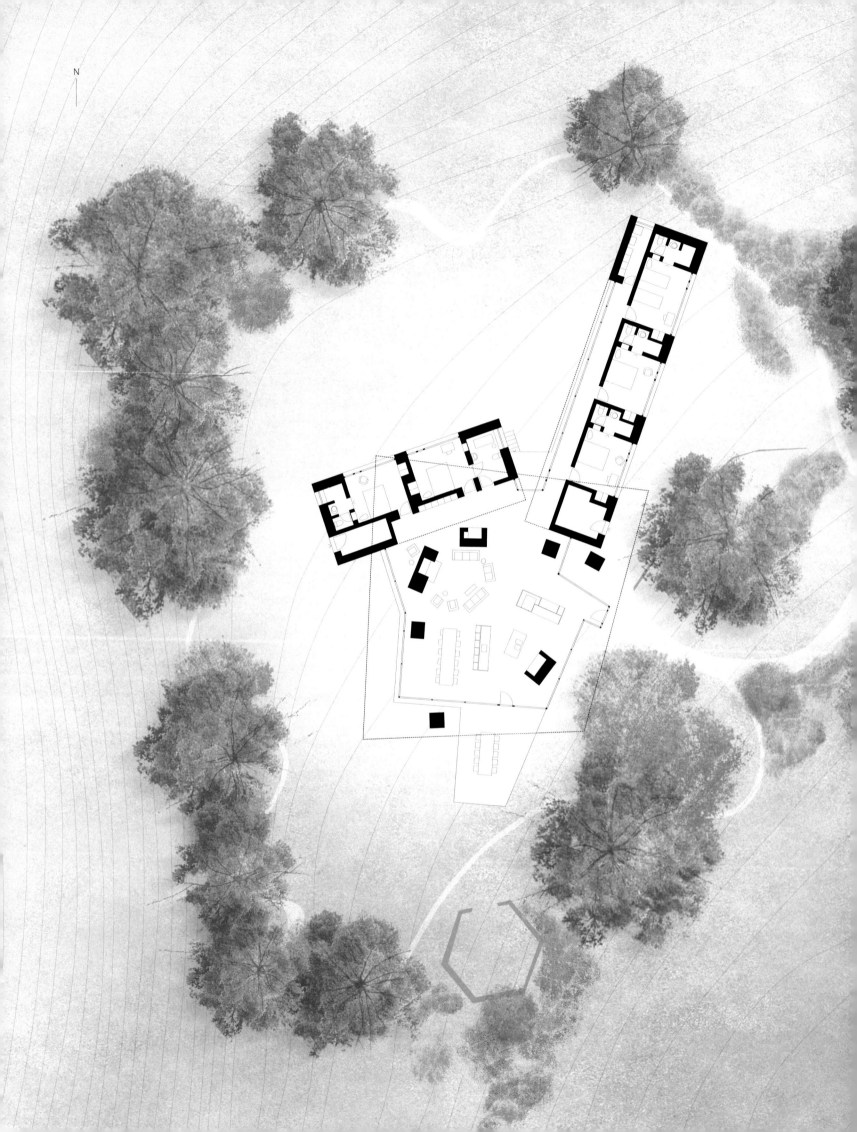

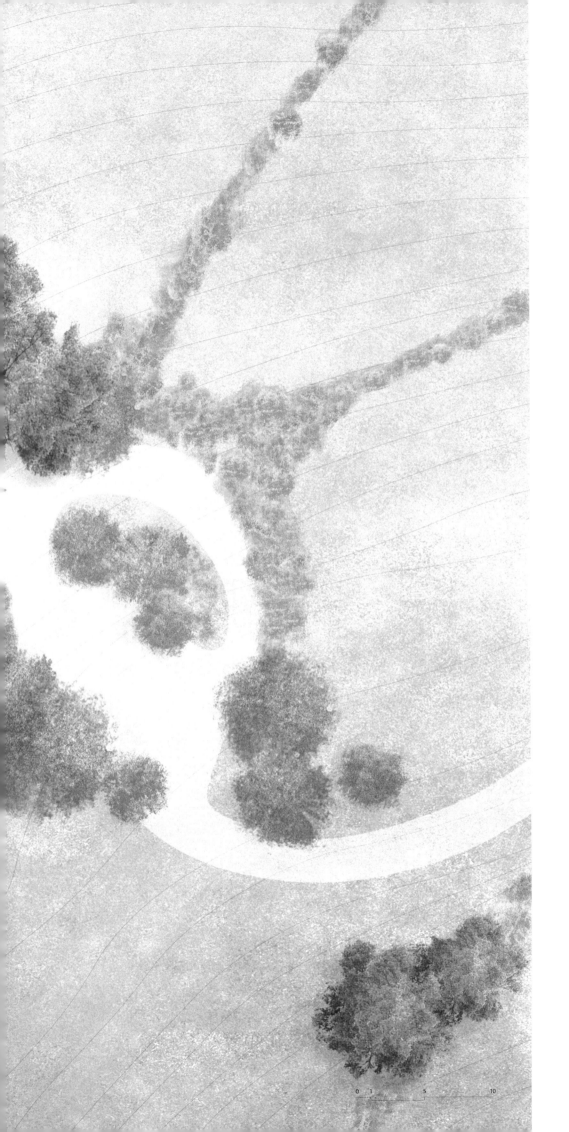

Los Angeles County Museum of Art, LACMA, Building for the
Permanent Collection, Los Angeles, California, USA
since 2008

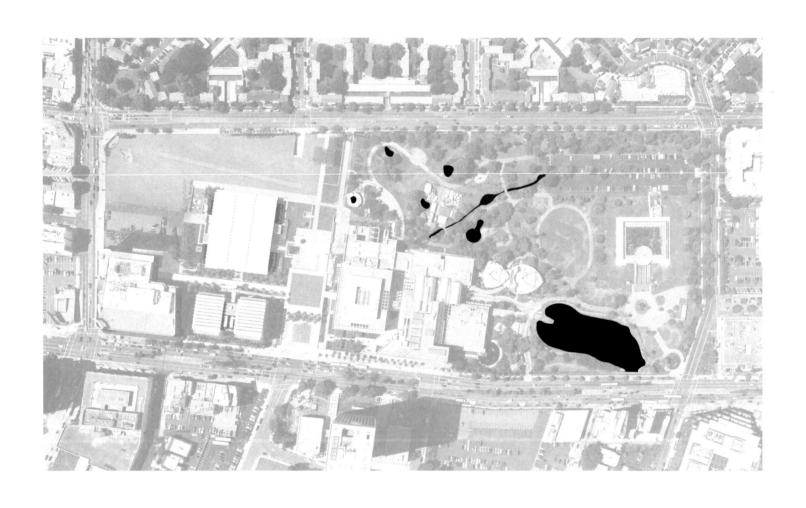

From an urban planning perspective, the development of the area where LACMA is located, Wilshire Boulevard in the Miracle Mile District of Los Angeles, presents a random and unstructured collection of open spaces and buildings that evolved through history. In the western part of this quarter, the corner of Wilshire Boulevard and Fairfax Avenue is dominated by the former May Company department store, a 1939 building preserved in its original Art Deco style and earmarked to house the Academy of Motion Pictures. Hancock Park to the east was originally an open space but is now partly occupied by buildings and a parking lot. Here are the famous La Brea Tar Pits, where pools of liquid asphalt come bubbling to the surface. The largest of these lies in the southeast corner of the site. In its immediate proximity is the Pavilion for Japanese Art by Bruce Goff and Bart Prince, completed in 1988, and another solitary construction, the Page Museum, devoted to the natural history of the location. The Page exhibits prehistoric finds from the area: bones of mammoths, saber-tooth tigers, and giant sloths that foundered and died in the sticky asphalt brew of the pools between ten and forty thousand years ago.

The central portion of the area is occupied by the buildings and grounds of the museum. This comprises Renzo Piano's Broad Contemporary Art Museum, built in 2008, consisting of two cube-shaped buildings for contemporary art; the Resnick Pavilion, inaugurated in 2010, which is a large, unobstructed and freely divisible space in the nature of a *Kunsthalle;* and some older museum buildings that were developed in two building phases. Old photographs of William Pereira's complex, finished in 1965, show architecture typical of that time. Pavilion-style building units create a loosely linked profile that is reflected in a pool of water. Additional buildings expanded the campus in 1986, overlaying and distorting the original composition beyond recognition.

Our client intends to create a new museum to replace this agglomeration of buildings in which the encyclopedic collection of the museum is preserved, curated, and exhibited. The art works are to be made more accessible and exhibited in new ways that will foster appreciation of the collection's significance.

Our design works with a large, freely undulating shape that responds organically to the historically evolved features of the location. It advances and retreats; it reacts to what is there; it creates contiguities with its neighbors, the Tar Pits, the Pavilion for Japanese Art, and Renzo Piano's exhibition buildings on the central plaza; it has a long arc sweeping down Wilshire Boulevard; it has a clear center of its own; and it functions as the focal point of the entire museum quarter. The horizontality of its large form echoes the great expanse and the wide horizon of the city. Seen from above it looks like a giant flower, an organic growth, nourished on historic soil. Perhaps it was always there, like the tar pits.

The museum collection will be shown on a single exhibition level that floats above the ground. It will be supported by voluminous, organically shaped plinths that will house spaces such as reception halls, an auditorium, a restaurant, as well as large display cases, spacious storage areas, curators' workrooms, and stairways and elevators to the upper level. These hollow units, encased in glass membranes, are set freely under the floating body of the museum that they support. They are transparent from within and without. The open area meandering between the plinths connects to the outdoor landscape of Hancock Park. The urban landscape of the neighborhood flows underneath the building.

The exhibition level is divided into various units corresponding to the collection's key areas. These are accessed through one or another of the plinth supports, depending on which part of the collection the visitor wants to see. The highlights of the collection will be on permanent display in the center of each unit. Arranged around these core spaces are various sequences of rooms with normal daylight or artificial lighting to meet the needs of temporary exhibitions.

The model pictured on page 68 shows a schematic rendering of the variations in the structure of the spaces. In the next phase of development we plan to link the units together organically. In the gaps between them we would like to install a network of corridors large enough to accommodate exhibits as well. A panorama gallery parallel to the long loop of the façade will run around the entire perimeter, connecting the internal passages and ensuring that there is always a view into the city for the visitor's orientation. The city is a constant presence.

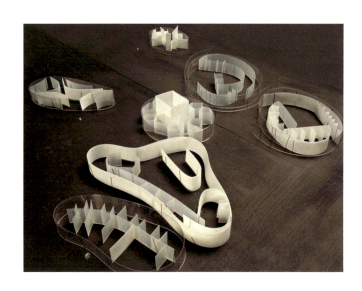

New City Gate with Theater and Café, Isny im Allgäu, Germany
2009–2012

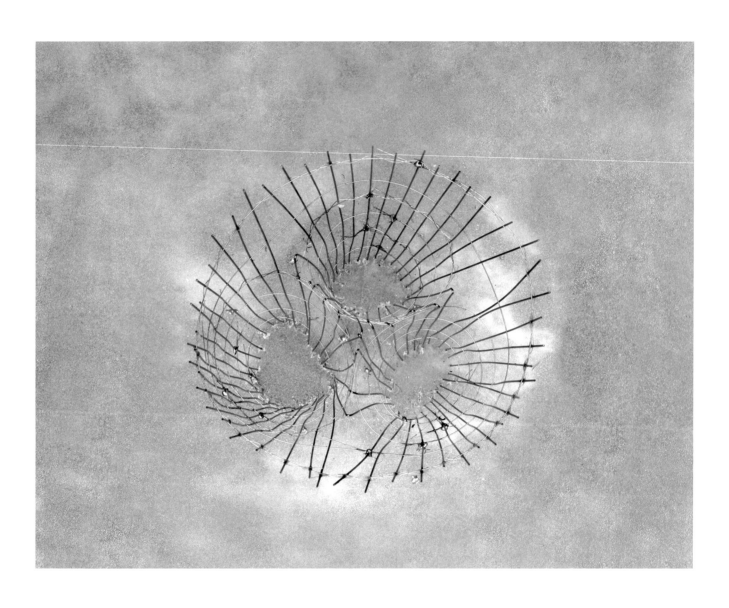

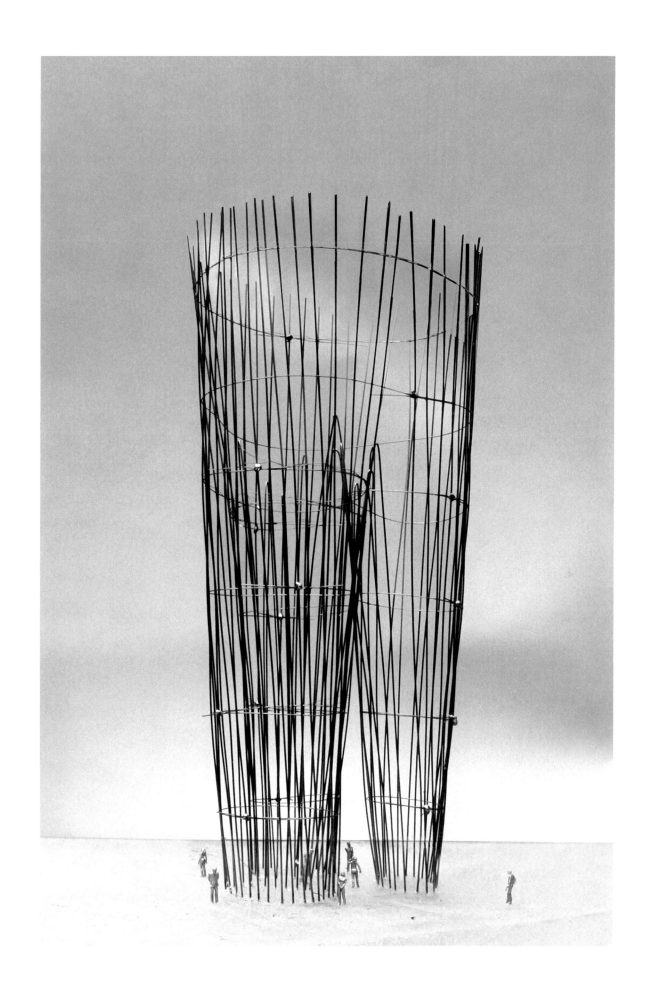

83

Isny in southern Germany is a city of towers. Its skyline features church steeples and the towers of the medieval fortifications. Our project proposes a new tower made of solid glass, to go alongside these historic towers and become, so to speak, a new member of their family.

The Obertor, or upper gate, occupied the site of our tower until 1830, when it was torn down to make way for through traffic. In recent times, however, a bypass has been built around Isny, so traffic no longer needs to squeeze through town. This led the town council to propose erecting a new tower where the old Obertor, also called the Lindauertor, once stood. There was talk of a new landmark for the town, a new selling point. The town's economy and culture would be invigorated. The shops, restaurants, and inns of the old center could do with a shot of energy—a stroll through the ancient alleys and streets makes this need apparent.

In view of these considerations, we worked with the civic authorities and other interested parties to develop a substantive plan before we even started designing the tower. Activities in the new building would radiate beyond the town and into the whole region. A special room for cultural functions would be built into the tower. We gave it the scale of a recital room with excellent acoustics. We began talking with people involved in music, theater, and literature, and explored means of collaborating with university-level institutions and academies, as we were convinced that the cultural resources required by such a project could not be provided by the town alone.

Then we designed the tower. We got in touch with glass brick manufacturers, procured material samples from Bohemia, used them to build model walls, and were pleased with the way the light was refracted by the glass. Working with civil engineer Joseph Schwartz we came up with a structural concept for the tower, which rises up on three pedestals merging into a large glass shell, with a sphere fitted into the top. This sphere is a lightweight steel structure. Its exterior is coated with silvery, fishlike scales, and inside it is paneled in dark wood. It houses the self-contained auditorium, with the foyer, bar, and restaurant directly underneath, from which the view looks out over the town and the expansive Allgäu landscape. The engineer Matthias Schuler showed us ways to cool and heat this literally unprecedented glass structure without wasting energy.

In time we felt that the design had coalesced. We had a clear vision of what would take place in the tower, and we developed its form from that.

Then we set up an exhibition in Isny for the townspeople, where we displayed our models and plans, and on two occasions explained and discussed our ideas to an audience of about a thousand people. We also had conversations with individuals potentially interested in financing the project, to prevent the municipal budget from being unduly burdened by building and maintaining the tower.

But just as the design won friends, it also found opponents. The town council decided to conduct a referendum and ask the public whether they wanted to have a new building erected on the site. A good sixty percent of the registered voters participated in the referendum, and a good seventy percent of them were opposed to pursuing the project.

A design—this has been my experience—that puts forward forms and structures not seen before arouses mistrust and fear. I experienced this in Berlin, in the little mountain village of Tschlin, in San Pedro de Atacama, and in other places. But I have come to realize over the years that the architectural ideas that occur to me in the course of working on a design are never really lost. They stay in the world and pollinate new work.

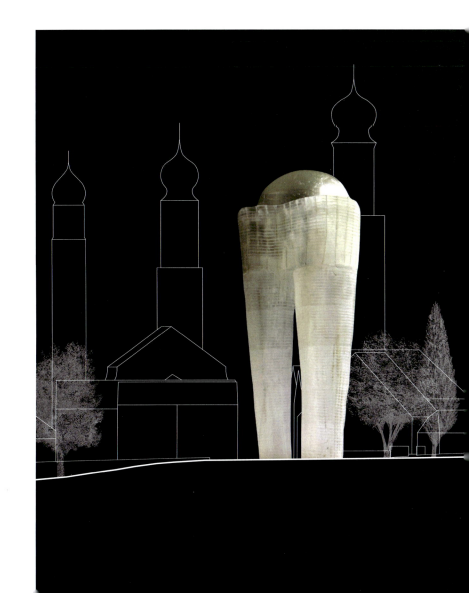

Adaptable Theater for Riom Castle, Riom, Graubünden
since 2009

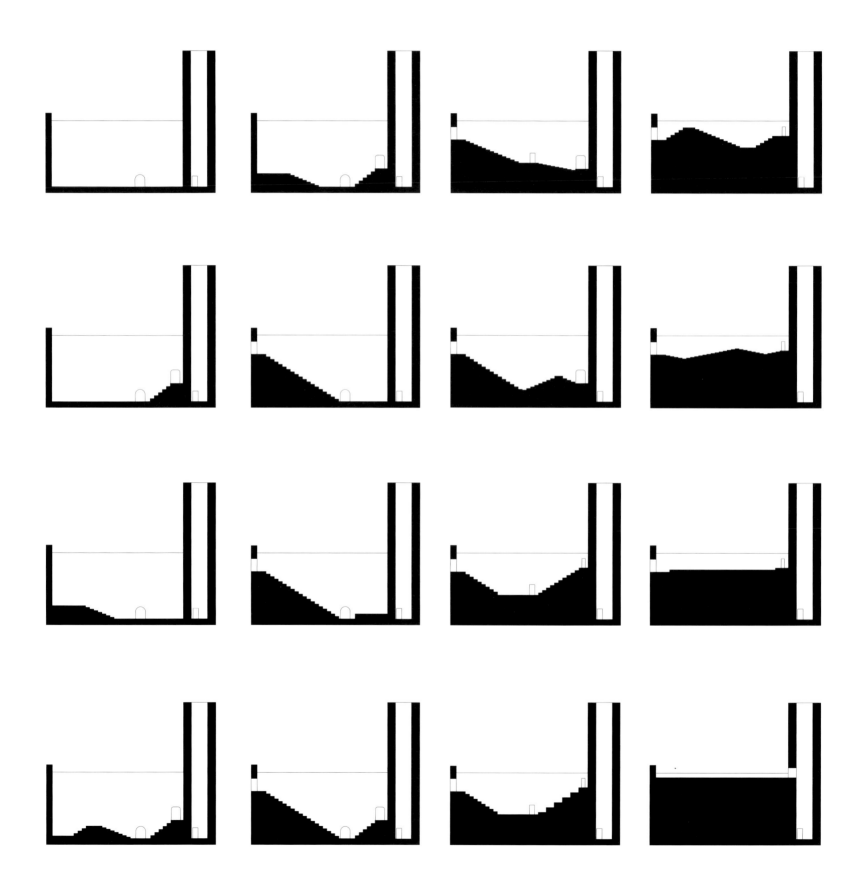

Origen is a festival in the mountains. It deals with language, theater, dance, and music, and through the person of its founder and director, Giovanni Netzer, it has a cultural affinity with the Alpine region of Oberhalbstein. The artistic activities of Origen are closely related to the landscape, the venues, and their history.

Origen's base of operations is Riom Castle. This fortress, now long a ruin, was built in the thirteenth century by the lords of Wangen-Burgeis. It sits high on a hill beneath the village of Riom for which it is named. To protect its ancient walls, a peaked roof was erected on top of the castle in 1973. The venue has been used by the Origen Festival since 2006. For this purpose, a conventional theater was installed inside the castle—an arrangement that Netzer considers interim. So he invited us to reconceive the whole interior of the castle as a theater space. The castle will foster Origen's goals.

The interior consists of a single space of impressive size: it is twenty-nine meters long, nine meters wide, and fourteen meters high. Our project will restore the open interior. The more recent installations will be removed, the roof taken off, and the space opened to the sky.

We have designed a movable stage floor for this space, consisting of thirty-two steel crossbeams that can be individually raised or lowered. This allows for a great many different performing and viewing situations from the flat floor at ground level, which affords a stunning experience of the inner space of the castle with its rectangle of night sky above, to undulating or canyon-like stage and counter-stage situations, right up to the flat floor just beneath the capstone level, which will become an open-air terrace.

The ancillary spaces needed for the theater will be kept to a minimum, housed in simple wooden buildings on the ground at the foot of the castle. The entrances for actors and audience, all original openings in the façade of the castle, are accessed by exterior stairs and bridges constructed in a manner similar to light scaffolding. They are reminiscent of the exterior wooden structures once built to access medieval fortresses.

A double pitched glass roof, replacing the former shingled roof, will protect the new theater space and the historic walls. However, it has additional functions: both halves can be opened up and folded out for specific performances. When the glass roof is closed, the walls inside the castle will be warmed by the sun as in a greenhouse, and will radiate their accumulated heat during an evening performance even when the roof is open. This means that the castle can also be used on cooler days. Because Origen is a summer festival, the building will not be heated; the historic masonry will not be touched: it belongs to the venue.

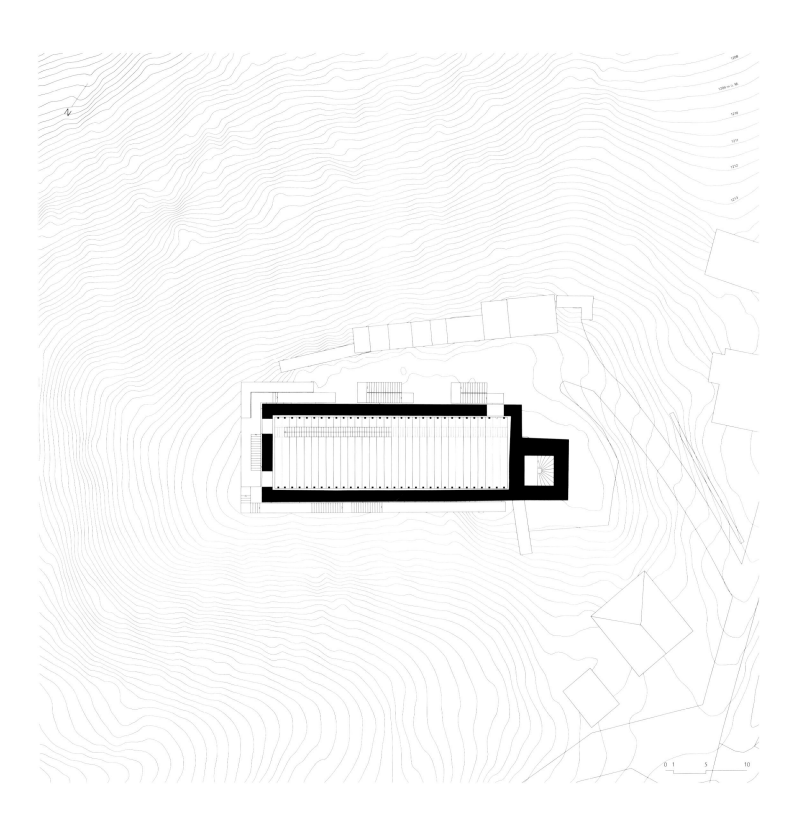

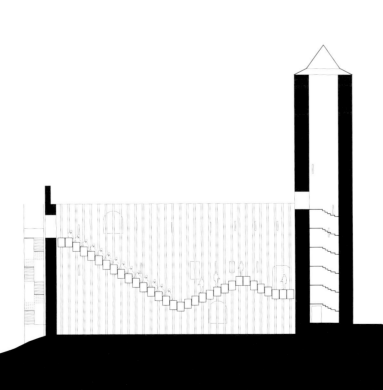

House of Seven Gardens, Doha, Qatar
since 2009

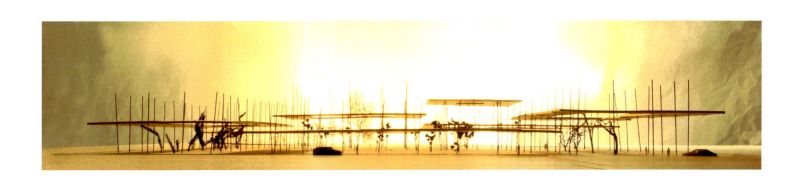

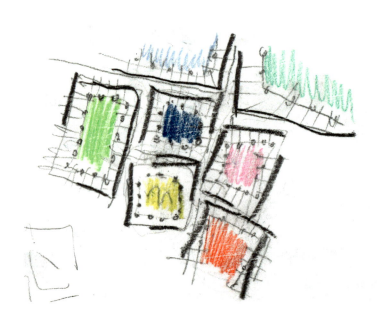

The house for Sheikh Saud Al Thani and his family is built like a little town. It offers many surprises, intimate paths, shaded spots, and concealed nooks. It is built around seven interior courtyards, each with a garden. The building screens off the world outside and creates its own quiet world.

It contains the private chambers of the Sheikh and the quarters reserved for the Sheikha, rooms where the women can be among themselves, others where the men meet, a kind of a drawing room in which the family receives official guests, a small art gallery, office spaces, and living quarters for men and women employees. In keeping with local tradition, these areas are all separate and distinct.

To meet these needs, the house is divided into seven sections, each with its own enclosed garden: a palm garden, sculpture garden, potted garden, water garden, desert garden, paradise garden, and shade garden. Cool materials, black wooden staves fashioned into grilles, fine fabrics, trees, bushes, flowers, grasses, scents, the sound of flowing water and footsteps on the floor, and a thousand and one gradations of light and shade: all these define the atmosphere of the house. The overall feeling is elegance. We dreamed of creating an appealing interplay of heaviness and lightness.

The connecting paths through the house run between the courtyards and adjoin one another as the need arises. The result is an overall rhythmic and dynamic design oriented toward the gardens in the interior. From outside, the house looks closed off in the traditional manner.

The largest of the seven gardens is the desert garden. It encompasses parts of an existing palm grove and is large enough to accommodate the Sheikh's traditional Bedouin tent. In the winter months, the tent is set up in the middle of the courtyard and is used to receive friends. An older, simple dwelling flanks the courtyard; this is his uncle's house, which the Sheikh treasures and intends to preserve. Another section of the courtyard border consists of a new "tent": a room built of stone and glass for the summer months when a traditional tent would be too hot.

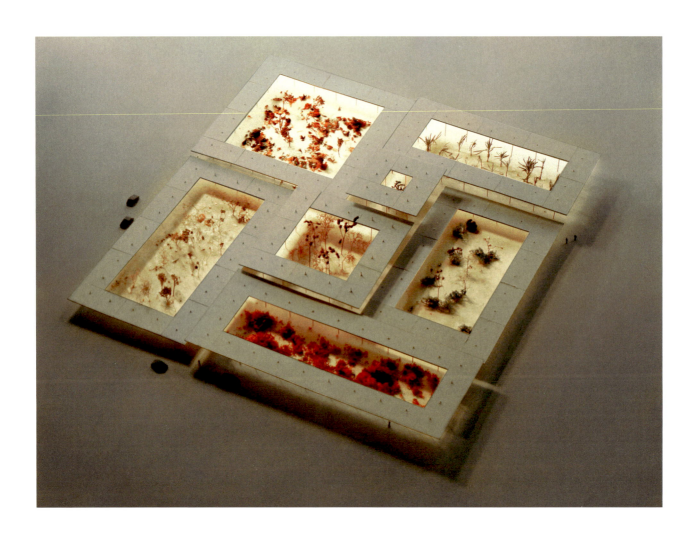

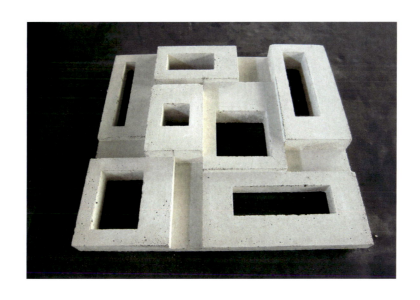

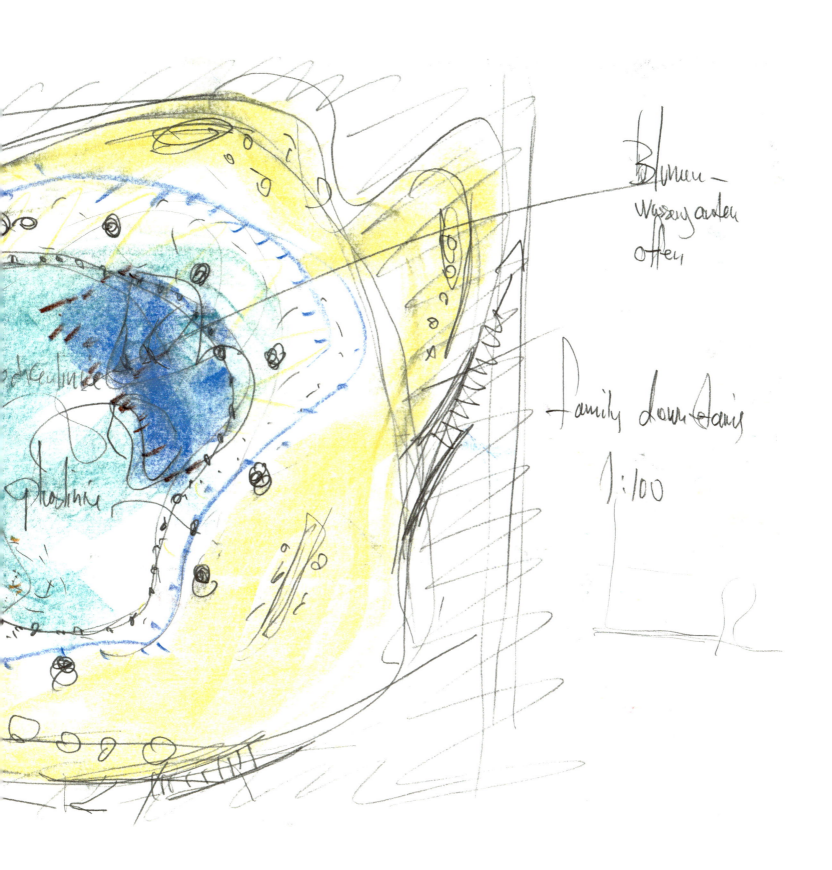

Blumen-
Wysenaden
offen

family downstairs
1:100

Serpentine Gallery Pavilion, London, England
2010 – 2011

I love fenced-in gardens, walled gardens, inner courtyards, garden courtyards. I love their intimacy, the sense of protection and sanctuary within a larger whole.

Creating a new temporary garden, a *hortus conclusus*, in London's Hyde Park—in other words, adding one more garden to a park that is already full of gardens—does that make sense? This question came up only at the very beginning of the design process, for we soon came to feel that visiting a wonderful garden in the architecture of our black, double-framed structure could offer a beautiful experience of tranquility and intimacy.

Our idea was to assemble visitors beneath an overhanging roof running all around a flower garden that would change from early summer right into autumn: the flowers blooming and fading, people coming and lingering by the plants, talking, drinking tea, reading a book, walking around, having a look at what is growing now. The atmosphere is peaceful.

We built the pavilion and the people enjoyed using it. I myself experienced it as a magnifying glass within the landscape of Hyde Park as a whole. The Serpentine Garden sharpened my view of the plant world and intensified my sense of growing, blooming, and fading that this intimate setting communicated to me.

Piet Oudolf created the garden. We gave him the frame, he gave it its heart.

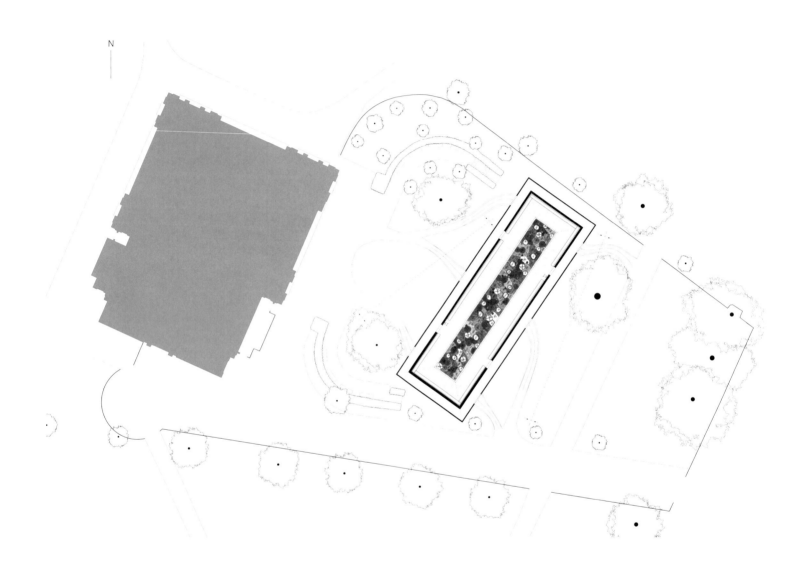

Perm State Art Gallery, Perm, Russia
since 2010

The collection of the Perm State Art Gallery is installed in the Church of the Transfiguration of Christ, built in 1832. In addition to the works on display, mainly paintings from the Western tradition, the collection contains an omnibus volume of about one thousand icons and many precious objects made of textiles, stone, metal, wood, and paper: largely folk art from the Perm region, most of which is kept in storage. There is also a significant collection of religious figures.

These wooden sculptures cast a spell on me the first time I saw them. The encounter was surprising. All crowded together and some only preserved in fragments, they are exhibited in a space sectioned off for them beneath the main vault of the former church: a seated figure of Christ, various saints, and groups of angels. Until recently—as I read in an informative volume by Marianne Stössl, *Verbotene Bilder* (Forbidden Images, Munich, 2006)—Western art history generally assumed that there were no figures of saints in Russia because the Orthodox Church forbade them. The Perm Museum corrects this false assumption quite impressively. The figures, some from the late eighteenth century, but most from the nineteenth, are anatomically realistic, smaller than life-sized, and polychrome. What they express seems to come from the depths of time. One thinks of folk art and peasant piety, of images of the divine found before the advent of Christianity in villages in the Ural Mountains, in the far reaches of the Russian East.

These figures in Perm were gathered together and saved from destruction in the 1920s in various expeditions to the villages of the region. Today they need a new home. The building that houses them, once a house of worship, is to be returned to the Russian Church, but to my mind there is another reason why they need a new home. The way they are exhibited today, one can see that they were uprooted from their native context in rural wooden churches and forcibly removed from their iconostases and their shrines. They stand there, naked and unprotected. A new museum would counteract this estrangement by placing the figures in appreciative, sympathetic surroundings, full of warmth and filled with shadows, light, and depth.

We have devised a particular spatial structure for the new Perm Museum and its collection. Just as a river meanders between rocks, so the visitor proceeds through the elongated building. An open exhibition passage leads between the volumes of the closed collection galleries. The passage moves back and forth, from the city side to the river side. The rooms on the city side are tall and windowless, reminiscent of churches with the light of the sun penetrating from above; on the opposite side they are low, with wide windows looking over the flowing waters of the Kama River out toward the north and into the vastness of the Russian landscape. Thinking about the project, we realize that wood has to play an important role in designing the exhibition spaces.

The new museum building, set into a topographical situation with exciting contrasts between the city and the riverscape, has a glassy iridescence. This solitary structure, conceived as a new part of the urban skyline, looks a little like a ship moored at the river side.

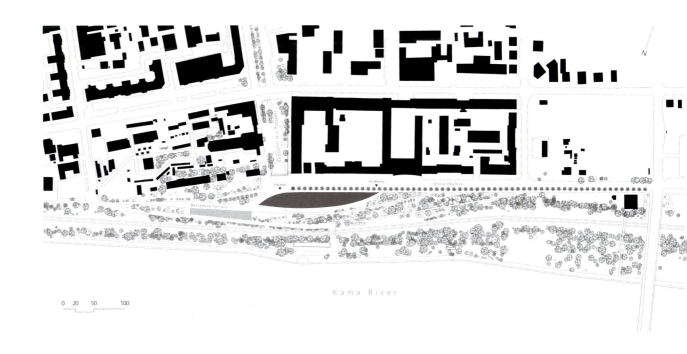

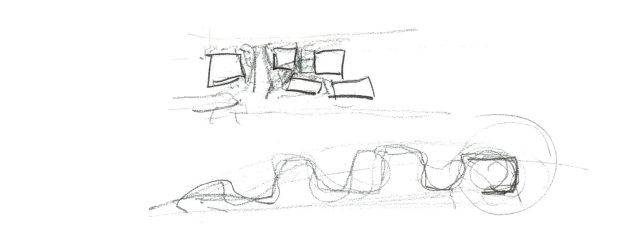

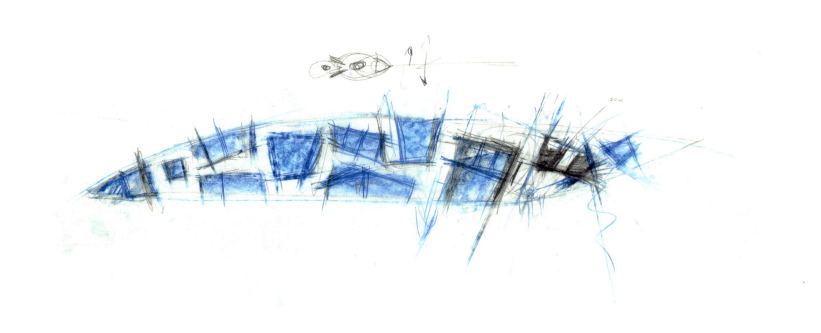

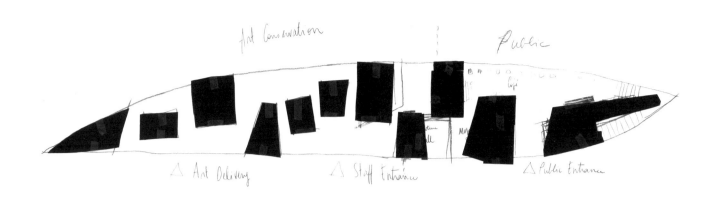

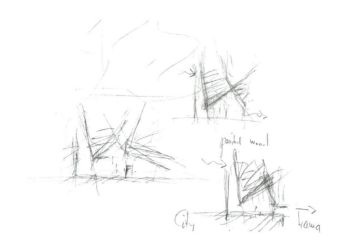

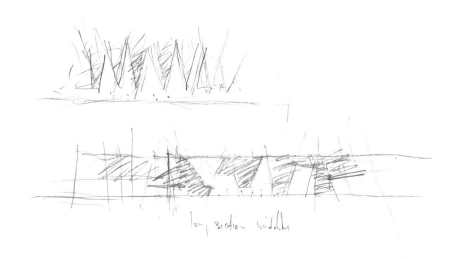

List of Works 1968–2013

Lämmern Hut, Swiss Alpine Club (SAC), Leukerbad, Wallis
Competition design 1968–1969

Residential Tower, Casti, Lumbrein, Graubünden
Project 1969, realization 1970
Expansion medieval tower

Café Demont, Vella, Graubünden
Project 1970, realization 1971
Remodeling

Dierauer House, Haldenstein, Graubünden
Project 1975, realization 1976

Damur House, Clugin, Graubünden
Project 1977, realization 1978
Restoration and expansion of historical complex

Founding of Atelier Zumthor 1978

San Vittore Service Area, Graubünden
Competition design 1978

Kleine Zapfholdern, Reigoldswil, Basel-Landschaft
Project 1979, realization 1979–1980
Conversion of barn

St. Nikolaus and Valentin Chapel, Vattiz, Graubünden
Restoration 1979–1982

District School, Churwalden, Graubünden
Competition 1979, project 1979–1982, realization 1982–1983
Extension
Collaboration and on-site management: Jürg Conzett;
frame structure: Toni Cavigelli with Walter Bieler;
art work: Hannes Vogel

Untervaz Community Hall, Graubünden
Competition design 1980

Bräm Farmer's Alpine Hut, Präz, Graubünden
Project 1980, realization 1980–1981
Replacement of old building

Urech Weekend House, Obersaxen, Graubünden
Project 1981

Räth House, two-family house with stable, Haldenstein, Graubünden
Project 1981–1983, realization 1983
Collaboration: Hansruedi Meuli and Marietta Walli;
frame structure: Melcherts + Branger AG; art work: Hannes Vogel

Malix Community Hall, Graubünden
Competition 1981, project 1982–1985, realization 1985–1986
Collaboration: Valentin Bearth (on-site management) and Jürg Conzett

Bündner Kunstmuseum Chur, Graubünden
Remodeling Villa Planta and Sulserbau, new walkway
In partnership with Peter Calonder and Hans-Jörg Ruch
Collaboration: Dieter Jüngling (on-site management),
Jürg Conzett, Andreas Hagmann, and Marcel Liesch;
art work: Hannes Vogel

Caminada House and Bakery, Vrin, Graubünden
Project building shell 1982–1984, realization by the client

Margadant House, Haldenstein, Graubünden
Project 1983–1984, realization 1984
Renovation
Collaboration and on-site management: Jürg Conzett;
frame structure: Jürg Buchli

Medical Practice Trepp/Bisaz, Chur, Graubünden
Renovation 1984
Collaboration and on-site management: Valentin Bearth

Haldenstein village center, Graubünden
Preliminary study 1984

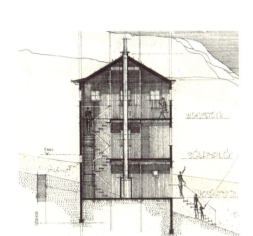

Egloff Weekend House, Tgamanada, Vrin, Graubünden
Project 1984

Rueun Community Hall, Graubünden
Competition design 1984
Collaboration: Valentin Bearth

Savognin Church Community Hall, Graubünden
Competition design 1984
Collaboration: Valentin Bearth, Hannes Vogel, and
Annalisa Zumthor-Cuorad

St. Valentin Chapel, Puzzatsch, Vrin, Graubünden
Project 1984–1985, realization 1985–1986
Restoration
Collaboration and on-site management: Valentin Bearth

Lumbrein Community Hall, Graubünden
Project 1984–1986, realization 1986–1987
Remodeling historical farmhouse
Collaboration and on-site management: Valentin Bearth;
frame structure: Jürg Buchli

Pontresina Community Hall, Graubünden
Competition design 1985
Collaboration: Valentin Bearth

Bener-Areal Housing Estate, Chur, Graubünden
Competition design 1985
Collaboration: Valentin Bearth

Atelier Zumthor, Haldenstein, Graubünden
Project 1985–1986, realization 1986
Collaboration: Reto Schaufelbühl; frame structure: Jürg Conzett;
art work: Matias Spescha
Volume 1, page 15

Shelter for Roman Archaeological Ruins, Chur, Graubünden
Project 1985–1986, realization 1986
Collaboration and on-site management: Reto Schaufelbühl;
frame structure: Jürg Buchli
Volume 1, page 35

Fontana House, Fidaz, Graubünden
Project 1985, realization 1985–1986
Renovation and expansion
Collaboration and on-site management: Valentin Bearth

Caplutta Sogn Benedetg, Sumvitg, Graubünden
Competition 1985, project 1985–1988, realization 1988
Collaboration and on-site management: Valentin Bearth and
Reto Schaufelbühl; geometry: Jürg Conzett; frame structure:
Jürg Buchli; art work: Jean Pfaff and Gieri Schmed
Volume 1, page 49

Sports Center, Arosa, Graubünden
Competition design 1986
Collaboration: Valentin Bearth

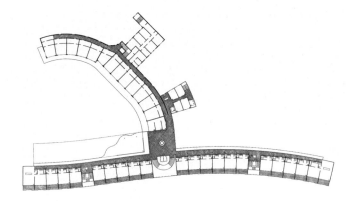

Hotel Therme and Thermal Bath, Vals, Graubünden
Invited study 1986, project 1987
Extension and remodeling
Collaboration on study: Valentin Bearth; collaboration on project:
Andreas Hagmann and Reto Schaufelbühl

Lugano Railroad Station, Ticino
Competition design 1987
Collaboration: Jürg Conzett, Andreas Hagmann, Dieter Jüngling, and
Reto Schaufelbühl; traffic engineer: Peter Hartmann

Gartengasse Riehen, Basel-Stadt
City planning competition design 1987
Collaboration: Valentin Bearth and Reto Schaufelbühl

Im Ried Community Hall, "Ramona," Landquart, Graubünden
Competition design 1987
Collaboration: Valentin Bearth, Andreas Hagmann, and
Reto Schaufelbühl

Spittelhof Housing Complex, Biel-Benken near Basel
Competition 1987, project 1989–1995, realization 1995–1996
Collaboration: Jürg Bumann (project manager),
Thomas Durisch, Marion Klein, and Marc Loeliger;
frame structure: Ingenieurgemeinschaft Affentranger + Müller and
Jürg Buchli
Volume 1, page 67

Rindermarkt Apartment Building and Shop, Zurich
Competition design 1988
Replacement of Rindermarkt 7
Collaboration: Andreas Hagmann and Dieter Jüngling
Volume 1, page 91

Landquart Railroad Station, Graubünden
Site development study 1989
Collaboration: Andreas Kaupp

Holiday Hotel, Swiss Association of the Blind, Willerzell, Schwyz
Competition design 1989
Collaboration: Andreas Hagmann, Dieter Jüngling, and
Reto Schaufelbühl

Business and Office Building, Wettingen, Aargau
Project 1989
Collaboration: Andreas Hagmann and Claire Moore

Burghalde Apartment Building, "Der reisende Krieger," Baden, Aargau
Competition design 1989
Collaboration: Andreas Hagmann, Dieter Jüngling, Marcel Liesch, and
Reto Schaufelbühl

Multipurpose Hall, Flond Schoolhouse, Graubünden
Competition design 1989
Collaboration: Andreas Hagmann, Dieter Jüngling, Marcel Liesch, and
Reto Schaufelbühl

Apartment Building "An der Stadtmauer," Jochstrasse, Chur,
Graubünden
Project 1989
Collaboration: Beate Nadler

Rothorn Mountaintop Restaurant and Gondola Station, "Steinway,"
Valbella, Graubünden
Invited study 1989–1990
Volume 1, page 99

Apartments for Senior Citizens, Masans, Chur, Graubünden
Competition 1989, project 1989–1991, realization 1991–1993
Collaboration: Martin Gautschi and Bruno Haefeli (on-site management), Thomas Durisch, Rolf Gerstlauer, Inger Molne, and Zeno Vogel; frame structure: Jürg Buchli; structural engineering: Ferdinand Stadlin; collaboration competition design expansion of nursing home and new apartment building for senior citizens: Dieter Jüngling, Andreas Hagmann, Marcel Liesch, and Reto Schaufelbühl
Volume 1, page 109

Bregenz Art Museum, Austria
Competition 1989, project 1990–1995, realization 1995–1997
Collaboration: Daniel Bosshard (project manager, museum building), Roswitha Büsser, Jürg Bumann, Katja Dambacher, Thomas Durisch, Marlene Gujan, and Thomas Kämpfer (project manager, administration building); frame structure: Robert Manahl; on-site management: Siegfried Wäger and Martin Zerlauth; HVAC: Meierhans + Partner AG; daylight facilities: Hanns Freymuth; collaboration competition design: Dieter Jüngling, Andreas Hagmann, and Reto Schaufelbühl
Volume 1, page 131

Schiesser House and Studio, Chur, Graubünden
Remodeling and expansion 1990
Collaboration: Marcel Liesch (on-site management), Andreas Hagmann and Dieter Jüngling

Gugalun House, Versam, Graubünden
Project 1990–1992, realization 1992–1994
Extension and remodeling
Collaboration and on-site management: Beat Müller and Zeno Vogel; frame structure: Jürg Conzett
Volume 2, page 7

Therme Vals, Graubünden
Project 1990–1994, realization 1994–1996
Collaboration: Marc Loeliger (project manager), Thomas Durisch, and Rainer Weitschies; frame structure: Ingenieurgemeinschaft Jürg Buchli and Casanova + Blumenthal; on-site management: Franz Bärtsch; structural engineering: Ferdinand Stadlin; HVAC: Meierhans + Partner AG; spa plumbing and heating: Schneider Aquatec AG; sound installation: Fritz Hauser
Volume 2, page 23

Schlössli Thusis, Graubünden
Remodeling kitchen 1991
Collaboration and on-site management: Beat Müller

Case study for new residential neighborhood in Cuncas, Sils, Graubünden
Competition design 1991
Collaboration: Thomas Durisch

St. Luzisteig Military Training Center, Maienfeld, Graubünden
Project 1991
Master plan for new room-and-board accommodation on the premises of the Baroque fortress
Collaboration: Thomas Durisch and Rolf Gerstlauer

Project for Residential Neighborhood, "Alte Brunnen," Igis, Landquart, Graubünden
Project 1991–1993
Collaboration: Beat Müller and Annette Ruf

Dim Lej Two-Family House, St. Moritz, Graubünden
Project 1992–1994
Collaboration: Thomas Durisch, Inger Molne, and Bodil Reinhardsen

Ice Skating Rink, Davos, Graubünden
Competition design 1992
Collaboration: Thomas Durisch

Topography of Terror, International Exhibition and Documentation
Center, Berlin, Germany
Competition 1993, project 1993–2003
Portions built in 1997 demolished by State of Berlin in 2004
Collaboration: Rainer Weitschies (project manager),
Gordian Blumenthal, Thomas Durisch, Maurus Frei, and Marlene
Gujan; frame structure: Ingenieurgemeinschaft Jürg Buchli and Herbert
Fink; on-site management: BAL Büro Am Lützowplatz GbR; structural
engineering: Ferdinand Stadlin; HVAC: Meierhans + Partner AG;
collaboration competition design: Jürg Bumann and Thomas Durisch
Volume 2, page 57

Apartment building on the outskirts of Jenins, Graubünden
Project 1994
Collaboration: Bodil Reinhardsen

European Academy of Bozen/Bolzano, Italy
Competition design 1995
Collaboration: Maurus Frei, Marlene Gujan, and Beat Müller

Swiss Embassy, Berlin, Germany
Invited study 1995
Remodeling and extension
Collaboration: Daniel Bosshard, Jürg Bumann, Thomas Kämpfer, and
Rainer Weitschies

Lindau Casino, Lake Constance, Germany
Competition design 1995
Collaboration: Jürg Bumann, Maurus Frei, Marlene Gujan,
Thomas Kämpfer, Beat Müller, and Rainer Weitschies

Residences with Studio, Krattenturmstrasse, Zurich
Project 1995
Collaboration: Thomas Kämpfer

Herz Jesu Church, Munich, Germany
Competition design 1996
Collaboration: Miguel Kreisler and Hannele Grönlund; liturgical
consultant: Daniel Schönbächler OSB
Volume 2, page 81

Lothar-Günther Buchheim Museum, Feldafing, Germany
Competition design 1996
Collaboration: Miguel Kreisler

Färberplatz Market Hall, Aarau, Aargau
Competition design 1996
Collaboration: Miguel Kreisler

Therme Vals and Hotel Therme Vals, Graubünden
Furniture design 1996–2005

Laban Centre for Movement and Dance, London, England
Competition design 1997
with Hannele Grönlund
Collaboration: Meritxell Vaquer i Fernàndez
Volume 2, page 91

Lichtforum Zumtobel Staff, Zurich
Project 1997
Collaboration: Daniel Schmid and Miguela Tamo

House of Design Production Nils Holger Moormann,
Aschau im Chiemgau, Germany
Project 1997
Collaboration: Marlene Gujan; frame structure: Jürg Conzett

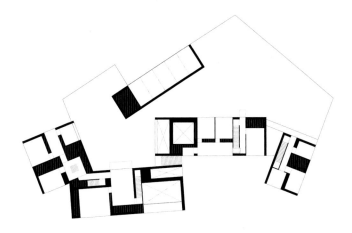

Villa in Küsnacht on Lake Zurich
Project 1997
Collaboration: Meritxell Vaquer i Fernàndez

Apartment Building, Bäumlihofareal, Basel
Project 1997
Collaboration: Marlene Gujan

Swiss Sound Box, Swiss Pavilion, Expo 2000, Hanover, Germany
Competition 1997, project 1998–1999, realization 2000
Collaboration: Rainer Weitschies (project manager), Uta Janina Graff, Kirsi Leiman, Stephan Meier, Curdin Michael, and Daniel Schmid; budget and scheduling: Franz Bärtsch; frame structure: Conzett Bronzini Gartmann AG; word curator: Plinio Bachmann; sound curator: Daniel Ott; gastronomy curator: Max Rigendinger; scenography consultant: Karoline Gruber; staff clothing curator: Ida Gut; communication: Lars Müller; journalist and writer: Peter Rüedi; filmmaker: Christoph Schaub; collaboration competition design: Daniel Bosshard
Volume 2, page 103

Luzi House, Jenaz, Graubünden
Project 1997–2001 (first project 1993–1995), realization 2001–2002
Collaboration: Michael Hemmi (project manager), Marlene Gujan, Simona Marugg, Curdin Michael, Daniel Schmid, and Rainer Weitschies; frame structure: Conzett Bronzini Gartmann AG
Volume 2, page 123

Kolumba Art Museum, Cologne, Germany
Competition 1997, project 1998–2003, realization 2003–2007
Collaboration: Rainer Weitschies (project manager), Mark Darlington, Reto Egloff, Mirco Elser, Rosário Gonçalves, Stephan Hausheer, Johannes Hunger, Oliver Krell, Simon Mahringer, Stephan Meier, Guy Muntwyler, Clemens Nuyken, Stefan Oeschger, Gian Salis, Daniel Schmid, Serge Schoemaker, and Thomas Ziegler; frame structure: Ingenieurgemeinschaft Jürg Buchli and Schwab & Partner; HVAC: Ingenieurbüro Gerhard Kahlert; structural engineering: Ferdinand Stadlin; landscape design: Peter Zumthor with Vogt Landschaftsarchitekten AG; collaboration competition design: Daniel Bosshard; copperplate printing: Peter Kneubühler
Volume 2, page 145

Burkard House, Bachenbülach, Zurich
Project 1998
Collaboration: Miguel Kreisler

Poetic Landscape, Bad Salzuflen, Germany
Project 1998–1999
Collaboration: Miguel Kreisler and Hannele Grönlund
Volume 3, page 7

Under Bongert, Haldenstein, Graubünden
Neighborhood design 1998–2000
Collaboration: Daniel Schmid

Broggini House, Vico Morcote, Ticino
Project 1998–2000
Collaboration: Miguel Kreisler

Zumthor House, Haldenstein, Graubünden
Project 1998–2003, realization 2003–2005
Collaboration: Michael Hemmi (project manager), Mirko Elser, Alexander Fthenakis, Stephan Hausheer, Pavlina Lucas, Csaba Tarsoly, and Michele Vassella; on-site management: Franz Bärtsch; frame structure: Conzett Bronzini Gartmann AG; structural engineering: Ferdinand Stadlin; heating and plumbing: Hans Hermann
Volume 3, page 21

Schwarz House, Chur, Graubünden
Project 1998–2005, realization 2005–2006
Collaboration: Michele Vassella (project manager), Stephan Hausheer,
Michael Hemmi, and Pavlina Lucas; on-site management:
Franz Bärtsch; frame structure: Conzett Bronzini Gartmann AG

Cloud Rock Wilderness Lodge, Moab, Utah, USA
Project 1999
Collaboration: Miguel Kreisler

Mountain Hotel, Tschlin, Graubünden
Project 1999–2002
Collaboration: Michael Hemmi, Miguel Kreisler, Pavlina Lucas,
and Rainer Weitschies; frame structure: Conzett Bronzini
Gartmann AG
Volume 3, page 47

Hotel Therme Vals, Graubünden
Remodeling and renovation 1999–2009
Blue Lounge, Red Restaurant, "Temporaries," Stucco Rooms, Therme
Shop, House Selva
Collaboration: Rainer Weitschies (project manager), Benjamin Bärtsch,
Stephan Hausheer, Philipp Imboden, Ruben Jodar, Miguel Kreisler,
Myriam Sterling, Florian van het Hekke, and Michele Vassella

Cornell University, Department of Architecture, Ithaca, New York, USA
Competition design 2000–2001
Collaboration: Mark Darlington, Reto Egloff, Michael Hemmi,
Sofie Hoet, Pavlina Lucas, Simona Marugg, Stephan Meier, and
Rainer Weitschies; frame structure: Conzett Bronzini Gartmann AG

I Ching Gallery, Dia Center for the Arts, Beacon, New York, USA
Project since 2000
Collaboration: Frank Furrer, Pavlina Lucas, Ruben Jodar,
Jesaias Kobelt, Miguel Kreisler, Eibhlín Ní Chathasaigh, and
Rainer Weitschies; art: 360° I Ching / 64 Sculptures, Walter de Maria;
HVAC: Ingenieurbüro Gerhard Kahlert; structural engineering:
Conzett Bronzini Gartmann AG; daylight technology: Institut für
Tageslichttechnik Stuttgart
Volume 3, page 63

Louise Bourgeois Pavilion, Dia Center for the Arts, Beacon, New York,
USA
Project 2001–2003
Collaboration: Miguel Kreisler and Pavlina Lucas

Harjunkulma Apartment Building, Jyväskylä, Finland
Project 2001–2004
Collaboration: Ivan Beer, Pekka Pakkanen, Csaba Tarsoly, and
Rainer Weitschies; frame structure: Conzett Bronzini Gartmann AG,
climate engineering: Ernst Basler + Partner AG
Volume 3, page 77

JP Williams Residence, Bedford, New York, USA
Project 2001–2004
Collaboration: Pavlina Lucas

Hotel Therme Vals, Vision 2005, Graubünden
Project 2001–2005
Collaboration: Ruben Jodar, Miguel Kreisler, Giacomo Ortalli,
Michele Vassella, Gaëlle Verrier, and Rainer Weitschies

Pingus Winery, Valbuena de Duero, Spain
Project 2001–2005
Collaboration: Ruben Jodar, Miguel Kreisler, and Pekka Pakkanen;
frame structure: Conzett Bronzini Gartmann AG
Volume 3, page 93

Bruder Klaus Field Chapel, Wachendorf, Germany
Project 2001–2005, realization 2005–2007
Collaboration: Frank Furrer (project manager), Rosário Gonçalves, Michael Hemmi, Ruben Jodar, Jesaias Kobelt, Niels Lofteröd, Pavlina Lucas, and Rainer Weitschies; frame structure: Jürg Buchli and Jung-Consult; lead flooring: Dagmar and Miroslav Stransky; bronze statue: Hans Josephsohn
Volume 3, page 109

Additional Cabins, Pension Briol, Barbian-Dreikirchen, Italy
Project since 2001
Collaboration: Lisa Barucco, Frank Furrer, Rosário Gonçalves, Stephan Hausheer, Michael Hemmi, Maximilian Putzmann, Rainer Weitschies, Christin Wüst, and Annalisa Zumthor-Cuorad; frame structure: Conzett Bronzini Gartmann AG and Schrentewein & Partner Srl
Volume 3, page 137

Pepper Mill
Manufactured since 2002 by Alessi, Crusinallo di Omegna, Italy

Stadtcafé Tübingen, Germany
Project 2002
Collaboration: Rainer Weitschies

Galerie Bastian, Berlin, Germany
Invited study 2002–2003
Collaboration: Pavlina Lucas and Rainer Weitschies
Volume 4, page 7

Kronberg Academy, Concert Hall, Kronberg im Taunus, Germany
Project 2002–2013
Collaboration: Rainer Weitschies

Redevelopment of De Meelfabriek, Leiden, Holland
Project since 2002
Collaboration: Rainer Weitschies (project manager), Ivan Beer, Nick Brennan Lobo, Frank Furrer, Gertjan Groen, Philipp Imboden, Daan Koch, Niels Lofteröd, Philippe Morel, Nikolai Müller, Eibhlín Ní Chathasaigh, Giacomo Ortalli, Anna Page, Julian von der Schulenburg, Louise Souter, Csaba Tarsoly, Gaëlle Verrier, Annalisa Zumthor-Cuorad, and Karol Zurawski
Volume 4, page 17

Bath House Aabach Estate, Risch, Zug
Project 2003–2005, realization 2005–2006
Restoration and remodeling
Collaboration: Frank Furrer (project manager), Gian Salis (on-site management), Mirco Elser, Jesaias Kobelt, Simon Mahringer, Michele Vassella, and Rainer Weitschies; frame structure: Conzett Bronzini Gartmann AG; structural engineering: Ferdinand Stadlin; landscape architecture: Vogt Landschaftsarchitekten AG; heating and plumbing: Hans Hermann

Klanghaus Schwendisee, Center for Sound and Music, Unterwasser, St. Gallen
Project 2003–2009
Collaboration: Rainer Weitschies

Summer Restaurant Insel Ufnau, Lake Zurich, Schwyz
Project 2003–2011
Collaboration: Ambra Fabi, Stephan Hausheer, Nikolai Müller, Guy Muntwyler, Gaëlle Verrier, Rainer Weitschies, and Annalisa Zumthor-Cuorad; frame structure: Conzett Bronzini Gartmann AG; gastronomy consultant: Max Rigendinger
Volume 4, page 35

Corporate Learning Center, Aabach Estate, Risch, Zug
Project 2003–2013
Collaboration: Rainer Weitschies (project manager), Tao Bärlocher, Duarte Brito, George Bunkall, Rico Bürkli, Marco Caminada, Frank Furrer, Philipp Imboden, Katarina Reinhold, Brigitta Ruff, Angelika Scheidegger, Julian von der Schulenburg, Gaëlle Verrier, Christin Wüst, Annalisa Zumthor-Cuorad, and Karol Zurawski; landscape architecture: Vogt Landschaftsarchitekten AG; frame structure: Dr. Schwartz Consulting AG; climate engineering: Transsolar Energietechnik GmbH; structural engineering: Zehnder & Kälin AG; HVAC: Aicher, De Martin, Zweng AG; wiring:Sytek AG; fire safety: Mario Fontana and Makiol + Wiederkehr
Volume 4, page 51

Almannajuvet Zinc Mine Museum, Sauda, Norway
Project 2003–2012, realization since 2012
Collaboration: Maximilian Putzmann (project manager), Lisa Barucco, Caroline Hammarström, Niels Lofteröd, Pavlina Lucas, Simon Mahringer, Sofia Miccichè, Stephan Schmid, Rainer Weitschies, and Annalisa Zumthor-Cuorad; frame structure: Finn-Erik Nilsen, Lauber Ingenieure, Jürg Buchli; on-site management: Inge Hoftun; graphic design and exhibition scenography: Aud Gloppen
Volume 4, page 73

Santa Giulia Church, Milan, Italy
Project 2005
Collaboration: Ambra Fabi and Francesco Garutti

Parco Termale e Galleria Urbana, San Pellegrino, Italy
Project 2005–2006
Collaboration: Ivan Beer, Guy Muntwyler, and Rainer Weitschies

Güterareal Residential Development, Lucerne
Competition design 2005–2006
Collaboration: Mirco Elser, Frank Furrer, Rosário Gonçalves, Stephan Hausheer, Guy Muntwyler, Clemens Nuyken, Gian Salis, Serge Schoemaker, Katrien Vertenten, and Rainer Weitschies; frame structure: Conzett Bronzini Gartmann AG; landscape architecture: Vogt Landschaftsarchitekten AG
Volume 4, page 91

A Tower for Therme Vals, Graubünden
Project 2005–2012
Remodeling of main building and Zerfreila Building
Collaboration: Ambra Fabi, Giacomo Ortalli, Gaëlle Verrier, and Rainer Weitschies
Volume 4, page 109

Felber House, Leis, Vals, Graubünden
Project 2006
Collaboration: Rosário Gonçalves

Leis Houses, Oberhus and Unterhus, Vals, Graubünden
Project 2006–2008, realization 2008–2009
Collaboration: Rosário Gonçalves (project manager), Lisa Barucco, Karina Bühler, Mengia Friberg, Simon Mahringer, Rainer Weitschies, and Annalisa Zumthor-Cuorad; frame structure: Jürg Buchli; structural engineering: Ferdinand Stadlin; heating and plumbing: Hans Hermann; artwork: Monika Bartholomé
Volume 4, page 121

Hisham's Palace, House of Mosaics, Jericho, Palestinian Territories
Project 2006–2010
Collaboration: Giacomo Ortalli, Gaëlle Verrier, and Rainer Weitschies; frame structure: Conzett Bronzini Gartmann AG
Volume 4, page 149

Kolumba Art Museum, Cologne, Germany
Furniture design 2007

Truffer House, Leis, Vals, Graubünden
Project 2007–2008
Remodeling
Collaboration: Karina Bühler and Peter Hutter

"Quality Vals," Graubünden
Development of the product "Therme Vals and Hotel Therme Vals"
2007–2010
Collaboration: Rainer Weitschies and Annalisa Zumthor-Cuorad

Steilneset Memorial to the Victims of the Witch Trials in the Finnmark,
Vardø, Norway
Project 2007–2009, realization 2009–2011
Collaboration: Rainer Weitschies and Simon Mahringer (project
managers), Lisa Barucco, Francesco Garutti, Maximilian Putzmann,
Gian Salis, and Annalisa Zumthor-Cuorad; on-site management:
Simon Mahringer and Svein Tore Dørmaenen; frame structure:
Finn-Erik Nilsen and Jürg Buchli; graphic design: Aud Gloppen;
art installation: Louise Bourgeois
Volume 4, page 163

Master Plan Hotel Therme Vals, Graubünden
Project 2007–2012
Collaboration: Lisa Barucco, Ambra Fabi, Giacomo Ortalli,
Gaëlle Verrier, and Rainer Weitschies

Hadspen House Observatory, Somerset, England
Project 2008

Nomads of Atacama Hotel, San Pedro de Atacama, Chile
Project 2008–2010
Collaboration: Gaëlle Verrier (project manager), Ambra Fabi,
Philipp Imboden, Giacomo Ortalli, and Annalisa Zumthor-Cuorad;
frame structure: Schlaich Bergermann & Partner
Volume 5, page 7

Bregenzerwald House of Craftsmanship, Andelsbuch, Austria
Project 2008–2012, realization 2012–2013
Collaboration: Rosário Gonçalves (project manager), Klemens Grund,
Daan Koch, Jordi Vilardaga, Rainer Weitschies, and Annalisa Zumthor-
Cuorad; on-site management: Wolfgang Elmenreich; frame structure:
Merz Kley Partner; climate engineering: Ingenieurbüro Gerhard Kahlert
with e²-energieberatung GmbH and Planungsteam E-Plus;
structural engineering: Erich Reiner; acoustics: Strauss
Elektroakustik GmbH
Volume 5, page 25

Chivelstone House, Devon, England
Project since 2008
Collaboration: Rainer Weitschies (project manager), Duarte Brito,
George Bunkall, Marco Caminada, Ambra Fabi, Klemens Grund,
Iris Hilton, Anna Page, Brigitta Ruff, Petra Stiermayr, Jordi Vilardaga,
Christin Wüst, and Annalisa Zumthor-Cuorad; on-site management:
Mole Architects; frame structure: Jane Wernick Associates;
structural and climate engineering: Transsolar Energietechnik GmbH;
HVAC: Integration; acoustics: Strauss Elektroakustik GmbH
Volume 5, page 43

Los Angeles County Museum of Art, LACMA, Building for the
Permanent Collection, Los Angeles, California, USA
Project since 2008
Collaboration: Karolina Slawecka (project manager),
Armina Alexandru, Ambra Fabi, Cecilia Marzullo, Sofia Miccichè,
Eibhlín Ní Chathasaigh, Giacomo Ortalli, Annika Staudt, Gaëlle Verrier,
and Annalisa Zumthor-Cuorad; frame structure:
Schlaich Bergermann & Partner; climate engineering:
Transsolar Energietechnik GmbH
Volume 5, page 61

Viewing Platform Lahti, Finland
Project since 2008
Collaboration: Ambra Fabi, Sarah Heidborn, and Annika Staudt;
frame structure: Jürg Buchli

Founding of Atelier Peter Zumthor & Partner AG with Rainer Weitschies
2009

Path lighting Vals, "Sentiero di Vals"
Manufactured in 2009 by Viabizzuno, Bentivoglio, Italy

Kunstmuseum Basel
Competition design 2009
Extension
Collaboration: Rosário Gonçalves, Gertjan Groen, Daan Koch, Nikolai Müller, Giacomo Ortalli, Anna Page, Giovanni Petrolito, Maximilian Putzmann, Annika Staudt, Gaëlle Verrier, Rainer Weitschies, and Annalisa Zumthor-Cuorad; frame structure: Jürg Buchli; structural engineering: Ferdinand Stadlin; climate engineering: Ingenieurbüro Gerhard Kahlert and e^2-energieberatung GmbH; lighting:
Reflexion AG; budget plan: Caretta & Weidmann Baumanagement AG

New City Gate with Theater and Café, Isny im Allgäu, Germany
Project 2009–2012
Collaboration: Nikolai Müller, Annika Staudt, Barbara Soldner, Rainer Weitschies, and Annalisa Zumthor-Cuorad; frame structure: Dr. Schwartz Consulting AG; climate engineering: Transsolar Energietechnik GmbH
Volume 5, page 79

Al-Rayyan Neighborhood Development, Doha, Qatar
Project since 2009
Collaboration: Ambra Fabi, Giacomo Ortalli, and Gaëlle Verrier

Adaptable Theater for the Origen festival, Riom Castle, Riom, Graubünden
Project since 2009
Collaboration: Giacomo Ortalli (project manager), Jann Erhard, Iris Hilton, Gaëlle Verrier, Rainer Weitschies, and Annalisa Zumthor-Cuorad; frame structure: Conzett Bronzini Gartmann AG; climate engineering: Transsolar Energietechnik GmbH; stage technology: Ernst J. Schulthess Planungsgruppe AB
Volume 5, page 95

House of Seven Gardens, Doha, Qatar
Project since 2009
Collaboration: Ivan Beer, Ambra Fabi, Pavlina Lucas, Sofia Miccichè, Giacomo Ortalli, and Gaëlle Verrier; specialized planning:
Arup Engineers
Volume 5, page 107

Kangia Icefjord Station, Illulissat, Greenland
Project since 2009
Collaboration: Annalisa Zumthor-Cuorad

Music Hotel in the Mountains, Braunwald, Glarus
Project since 2009
Collaboration: Iris Hilton, Barbara Soldner, and Annalisa Zumthor-Cuorad

Maguire House, Westwood, Los Angeles, California, USA
Project since 2009
Collaboration: Karolina Slawecka (project manager), Armina Alexandru, Ambra Fabi, Eibhlín Ní Chathasaigh, Cecilia Marzullo, Anna Page, Petra Stiermayr, and Annalisa Zumthor-Cuorad

Glassware
Project since 2010 for Alessi, Crusinallo di Omegna, Italy
Collaboration: Iris Hilton, Sofia Miccichè, and Annalisa Zumthor-Cuorad

Landscape Hotel Alp Bidanätsch, Vals, Graubünden
Project 2010–2011
Collaboration: Ivan Beer, Petra Stiermayr, and Annalisa Zumthor-Cuorad

Serpentine Gallery Pavilion, London, England
Project 2010–2011, realization 2011
Collaboration: Anna Page (project manager), Klemens Grund,
Petra Stiermayr, and Annalisa Zumthor-Cuorad; frame structure,
lighting and fire safety: Arup Engineers; garden design: Piet Oudolf
Volume 5, page 123

Süsswinkel Neighborhood Development Plan, Haldenstein,
Graubünden
Project 2010–2012
Collaboration: Marco Caminada

Türmlihus, Leis, Vals, Graubünden
Project 2010–2012, realization 2013
Collaboration: Samuel Smith (project manager), Marco Caminada,
Mengia Friberg, Rosário Gonçalves, Brigitta Ruff, and
Rainer Weitschies; frame structure: Giachen Blumenthal and
Jon Andrea Könz; structural engineering: Martin Kant; heating and
plumbing: Hesaplan AG; artwork: Monika Bartholomé

Am Dorfplatz Apartment Building, Haldenstein, Graubünden
Project since 2010
Collaboration: Gertjan Groen, Eibhlín Ní Chathasaigh, Brigitta Ruff,
Karolina Slawecka, and Annalisa Zumthor-Cuorad

Nowy Teatr Kielce, Poland
Project since 2010
Collaboration: Karol Zurawski

Perm State Art Gallery, Perm, Russia
Project since 2010
Collaboration: Ivan Beer, Eibhlín Ní Chathasaigh, Marion Dufat,
Benjamin Groothuijse, Iris Hilton, Sofia Miccichè, Karolina Slawecka,
and Karol Zurawski
Volume 5, page 139

New Atelier Süsswinkel 17, Haldenstein, Graubünden
Project 2011–2013, realization 2013–2014
Collaboration: Rico Bürkli, Marco Caminada, Rosário Gonçalves,
Gertjan Groen, Brigitta Ruff, Annika Staudt, and Rainer Weitschies;
frame structure: Plácido Pérez; structural engineering: Martin Kant;
climate engineering: Transsolar Energietechnik GmbH; HVAC:
Willi Haustechnik AG

ECM Temporary Concert Hall, Haus der Kunst, Munich, Germany
Project 2012
Collaboration: Karolina Slawecka (project manager),
Eibhlín Ní Chathasaigh, and Jordi Vilardaga;
climate engineering: Transsolar Energietechnik GmbH;
acoustics: Strauss Elektroakustik GmbH

Los Angeles County Museum of Art, LACMA, Museum House,
Los Angeles, California, USA
Project since 2013
Collaboration: Eibhlín Ní Chathasaigh and Karolina Slawecka

Texts by Peter Zumthor

Vrin, Lugnez. Siedlungsinventar Graubünden, in collaboration with Johanna Strübin Rindlisbacher et al., Kantonale Denkmalpflege Graubünden, Chur 1976

Vicosoprano. Entwicklung eines gestalterischen Grundgerüstes für eine Bauzone mit privaten Einfamilienhäusern am Dorfrand: Fallbeispiel, Baugestaltung in den Regionen, Bündner Vereinigung für Raumplanung, Chur 1980

Dorfplatz Vrin. Vorschläge zur Pflege und Sanierung der historischen Bausubstanz, Haldenstein 1981

Siedlungs-Inventarisation in Graubünden. Aufgabenstellung und Methode des Bündner Siedlungsinventares, mit Inventar Castasegna, Kantonale Denkmalpflege Graubünden, Chur 1981

Neues Bauen im alpinen Kontext, with Dorothee Huber, offprint from Unsere Kunstdenkmäler 35/1984, no. 4, Gesellschaft für Schweizerische Kunstgeschichte, Bern 1984

Partituren und Bilder. Architektonische Arbeiten aus dem Atelier Peter Zumthor, 1985–1988, photographs by Hans Danuser, exh. cat. Architekturgalerie Luzern (October 2–23, 1988), Haus der Architektur Graz (July 27–August 18, 1989), Architekturgalerie Luzern, Lucerne 1988, 2nd ed. 1994

Architekturworkshop 1989. Peripherie, 27.7.–16.3., Haus der Architektur Graz, Leuschner & Lubensky, Graz 1989

Eine Anschauung der Dinge. Über die Sprache der Architektur, Haldenstein 1992 [text reprinted in *Thinking Architecture*]

Kunsthaus Bregenz—Versuch, einen noch nicht abgeschlossenen Entwurf einmal mehr zu Ende zu denken, in Uta Brandes, Kunst im Bau, Kunst- und Ausstellungshalle der Bundesrepublik Deutschland, Schriftenreihe Forum, vol. 1, Steidl, Göttingen 1994, pp. 106–11

Stabwerk. Internationales Besucher- und Dokumentationszentrum "Topographie des Terrors," Berlin, exh. cat. Aedes, Galerie und Architekturforum (December 6, 1995–February 4, 1996), Aedes, Berlin 1995

Thermal Bath at Vals, exh. cat. Architectural Association London (February 16 – March 22, 1996), Exemplary Projects 1, Architectural Association, London 1996

Der Neubau des Erzbischöflichen Diözesanmuseums. Gedanken zum Entwurf, in Kolumba. Ein Architekturwettbewerb in Köln 1997, Erzbischöfliches Diözesanmuseum Köln, Walther König, Cologne 1997, pp. 126–27

Three Concepts. Thermal Bath Vals, Art Museum Bregenz, "Topography of Terror" Berlin, exh. cat. Architekturgalerie Luzern (September 28 – November 2, 1997), Edition Architekturgalerie Luzern, Birkhäuser, Basel/Boston/Berlin 1997
Drei Konzepte, Birkhäuser, Basel/Boston/Berlin 1997 [Ger.]

Kunsthaus Bregenz, texts by Peter Zumthor and Friedrich Achleitner, photographs by Hélène Binet, ed. by Edelbert Köb and Kunsthaus Bregenz, archiv kunst architektur, Werkdokumente, Gerd Hatje, Stuttgart 1997

A Way of Looking at Things, in Peter Zumthor, ed. by Nobuyuki Yoshida, texts by Friedrich Achleitner, Hiroshi Nakao, and Peter Zumthor, photographs by Shigeo Ogawa, a+u Publishing, Tokyo 1998, special edition February 1998, pp. 6–25 [En./Jp.]

Peter Zumthor—Works. Buildings and Projects 1979–1997, photographs by Hélène Binet, Lars Müller, Baden 1998, 2nd ed. Birkhäuser, Basel/Boston/Berlin 1999
Peter Zumthor—Häuser, 1979–1997, Lars Müller, Baden 1998, 2nd ed. Birkhäuser, Basel/Boston/Berlin 1999 [Ger.]

Wörter, Häuser, Gegend. Zur Gestaltung der Poetischen Landschaft, in Poetische Landschaft—Die Orte der Gedichte, texts by Amanda Aizpuriete et al., ed. by Brigitte Labs-Ehlert and Peter Zumthor, Literaturbüro Ostwestfalen-Lippe / Der Regionale Heilgarten, Bad Salzuflen 1999

Swiss Sound Box. A Handbook for the Pavilion of the Swiss Confederation at Expo 2000 in Hanover, with Plinio Bachmann et al., ed. by Roderick Hönig, Birkhäuser, Basel/Boston/Berlin 2000
Klangkörperbuch. Lexikon zum Pavillon der Schweizerischen Eidgenossenschaft an der Expo in Hannover, Birkhäuser, Basel/Boston/Berlin 2000 [Ger.]
Corps sonore suisse. Lexique du pavillon de la Confédération helvétique pour l'Expo 2000 à Hanovre, Birkhäuser, Basel/Boston/Berlin 2000 [Fr.]

Häuser für Gedichte, in Wer Eile hat, verliert seine Zeit. Raum für Sprache, Raum für Literatur. Die Poetische Landschaft. IX. Literaturbegegnung Schwalenberg 2001, ed. by Brigitte Labs-Ehlert, Literaturbüro Ostwestfalen-Lippe, Detmold 2001, pp. 79–85

Make it typical! A small atlas of architectural atmosphere, ed. by Atelier Zumthor and Accademia di architettura, Accademia di architettura, Mendrisio 2005

Ciao Chiasso. Interventi per la doppia periferia, ed. by Atelier Zumthor and Accademia di architettura, Accademia di architettura, Mendrisio 2005

Zumthor. Spirit of Nature Wood Architecture Award 2006, Wood in Culture Association, Rakennustieto Oy, Helsinki 2006, 2nd ed. 2007

Wieviel Licht braucht der Mensch, um leben zu können, und wieviel Dunkelheit?—Di quanta luce ha bisogno l'uomo per vivere e di quanta oscurità? Peter Zumthor, Ivan Beer et al., Accademia di architettura dell'Università della Svizzera italiana, Studies on Alpine History, vol. 3 (Nationales Forschungsprogramm 48 "Landschaften und Lebensräume der Alpen"), Vdf Hochschulverlag an der ETH Zürich, Zurich 2006

Zwischen Bild und Realität, Peter Noever, Ralf Konersmann, and Peter Zumthor, Architekturvorträge der ETH Zürich, no. 2, gta Verlag, Zurich 2006

Atmospheres. Architectural Environments—Surrounding Objects, Birkhäuser, Basel/Boston/Berlin 2006
Atmosphären. Architektonische Umgebungen—Die Dinge um mich herum, Birkhäuser, Basel/Boston/Berlin 2006 [Ger.]
Atmósferas. Entornos arquitectónicos—Las cosas a mi alrededor, G. Gili, Barcelona 2006, 2nd ed. 2009 [Sp.]
Atmosferas. Entornos arquitectónicos—As coisas que me rodeiam, G. Gili, Barcelona 2006, 2nd ed. 2009 [Pt.]
Atmosfere. Ambienti architettonici. Le cose che ci circondano, Electa, Milano 2007 [It.]
Atmosphères. Environnements architecturaux. Ce qui m'entoure, Birkhäuser, Basel/Boston/Berlin 2008 [Fr.]

Peter Zumthor Therme Vals, texts by Sigrid Hauser and Peter Zumthor, photographs by Hélène Binet, Scheidegger & Spiess, Zurich 2007, 2nd ed. 2008, 3rd ed. 2011
Peter Zumthor Therme Vals, Scheidegger & Spiess, Zurich 2007 [Ger.]
Peter Zumthor Therme Vals, Infolio, Gollion 2007 [Fr.]

In der Lehre, in: Neue Zürcher Zeitung, No. 68, March 22/23, 2008, B2 (Literatur und Kunst)

Thinking Architecture, Lars Müller, Baden 1998, 2nd expanded ed., Birkhäuser, Basel/Boston/Berlin 2006, 3rd additionally expanded ed., Birkhäuser, Basel/Boston/Berlin 2010
Architektur denken, Lars Müller, Baden 1998, reprint 1999, 2nd expanded ed., Birkhäuser, Basel/Boston/Berlin 2006, 3rd additionally expanded ed., Birkhäuser, Basel/Boston/Berlin 2010 [Ger.]
Penser l'architecture, Birkhäuser, Basel/Boston/Berlin 2008, 2nd expanded ed., 2010 [Fr.]
Pensar la arquitectura, G. Gili, Barcelona 2004, 2nd expanded ed., 2009 [Sp.]
Pensar a arquitectura, G. Gili, Barcelona 2005, 2nd expanded ed., 2009 [Pt.]
Pensare architettura, Lars Müller, Baden 1998, 2nd expanded ed., Electa, Milan 2003, reprint 2004 [It.]
Misliti arhitekturu, AGM, Zagreb 2003 [Croat.]
Promýšlet architekturu, Archa, Zlín 2009 [Czech]
Myślenie architekturą, Karakter, Kraków 2010 [Polish]
建築を考える *(Kenchiku o kangaeru),* Misuzu Shobo, Tokyo 2012, special edition 2013 [Jp.]

Hommage für Duri und Clara, in: Graubünden im Bild. Die Fundaziun Capauliana, ed. by Marco Obrist, Chur 2003, pp. 139–43 (reprinted in Peter Egloff, Der Bischof als Druide. Berichte aus Graubünden, with a postscript by Köbi Gantenbein, Desertina, Chur 2013, pp. 173–79)

Das Haus, Tony Fretton, Peter Zumthor, and Roger Diener, Architekturvorträge der ETH Zürich, no. 9, gta Verlag, Zurich 2010

Erste Häuser, erste Räume, in: Das Haus. Ein Bericht, text by Walter Morgenthaler, photogrpahs by Ute Schendel, Vexer, St. Gallen 2011, pp. 5–6

Steilneset minnested. Til minne om de trolldomsdømte i Finnmark / Steilneset Memorial. To the Victims of the Finnmark Witchcraft Trials, Louise Bourgeois and Peter Zumthor, Forlaget Press in collaboration with The Norwegian Public Roads Administration, National Tourist Routes in Norway, Oslo 2011

Peter Zumthor. Hortus Conclusus. Serpentine Gallery Pavilion 2011, ed. by Sophie O'Brien et al., exh. cat. Serpentine Gallery, London (July 1 – October 16, 2011), Koenig Books, London 2011

Die Architektur und ihr Transfer in den Bild-Raum, ausgehend vom gemeinsamen Projekt Partituren und Bilder, sowie Gedanken zu Darstellungsmöglichkeiten von Architektur, in: Die Neuerfindung der Fotografie. Materialien und Analysen sowie Gespräche von Hans Danuser mit Bettina Gockel, Reto Hänny, Philip Ursprung und Peter Zumthor, ed. by Bettina Gockel and Hans Danuser, Studies in Theory and History of Photography, vol. 4, Walter de Gruyter, Berlin 2014

Biography

Peter Zumthor, born 1943, grew up in Oberwil near Basel. After completing an apprenticeship as a cabinetmaker, studied interior design, design and architecture at the School of Arts and Crafts in Basel and at the Pratt Institute in New York. Worked for ten years at the Historical Preservation Society of Canton Graubünden. 1978 established his architectural office in Haldenstein, Switzerland. 1996–2008 Professor at the Accademia di Architettura der Università della Svizzera italiana, Mendrisio. Visiting professor at several universities, such as the Harvard Graduate School of Design.
Peter Zumthor has received numerous prizes, including the world's most prestigious architectural awards: Mies van der Rohe Award for European Architecture (1998), Japanese Praemium Imperiale (2008), Pritzker Architecture Prize (2009), and the Royal Gold Medal of the Royal Institute of British Architects (2012), and in 2009 was made a Foreign Honorary Member of the American Academy of Arts and Sciences.

Collaborators 1985–2013

David Agudo, Jämy Ahadi, Armina Alexandru, Timo Allemann, Logan Allen, Kevin Barden, Tao Bärlocher, Benjamin Bärtsch, Lisa Barucco, Valentin Bearth, Ivan Beer, Katharina Benjamin, Jean Besson, Amalie Bleibach, Gordian Blumenthal, Daniel Bosshard, Katja Bräunig, Nick Brennan Lobo, Duarte Brito, Karina Bühler, Jürg Bumann, George Bunkall, Rico Bürkli, Roswitha Büsser, Bea Calzaferri Gianotti, Marco Caminada, Nicole Caminada, Laura Claire Cannon, Rosinda Casais, Susanne Ciseri, Conradin Clavuot, Göri Clavuot, Marisia Conn, Margrith Contesse-Truog, Jürg Conzett, Jaume Crespi Quintana, Paul Curschellas, Claudine Dällenbach, Katja Dambacher, Mark Darlington, Iris Dätwyler, Séverin De Courten, Magdalena Decurtins-Stecher, Andrea Deplazes, Remo Derungs, Ruth Desax Ba, Tom Dowdall, Marion Dufat, Thomas Durisch, Jadranka Dzinic, Reto Egloff, Thale Eidheim, Murat Ekinci, Mirco Elser, Tiziana Epifani, Jann Erhard, Ambra Fabi, Felipe Fankhauser, Donatella Fioretti, Sophie Frank, Maurus Frei, Mengia Friberg, Ueli Frischknecht, Alexander Fthenakis, Frank Furrer, Francesco Garutti, Joan Gaudin, Martin Gautschi, Thomas Gebert, Rolf Gerstlauer, Janna Göldi, Rosário Gonçalves, Uta Janina Graff, Joos Gredig, Gertjan Groen, Benjamin Groothuijse, Klemens Grund, Marlene Gujan, Bruno Haefeli, Andreas Hagmann, Caroline Hammarström, Mads Hansen, Gideon Hartmann, Stephan Hausheer, Sarah Heidborn, Michael Hemmi, Iris Hilton, Carolin Hinne, Stefanie Hitz, Sofie Hoet, Stefan Höhn, Matthew Howell, Johannes Hunger, Peter Hutter, Philipp Imboden, Miriam Janssen, Matthew Jarvis, Johann Gaudenz Jehli, Ruben Jodar, Franco Joos, Rodrigo Jorge, Dieter Jüngling, Thomas Kämpfer, Eva Maria Kampichler, Andreas Kaupp, Thomas Keller, Wolfram Kill, Ki Jun Kim, Marion Klein, Jesaias Kobelt, Daan Koch, Bence Kollar, Miguel Kreisler, Oliver Krell, Nora Küenzi, Nathalie Kupferschmid, Bettina Lareida, Kirsi Leiman, Marcel Liesch, Marc Loeliger, Niels Lofteröd, Bernardo Lopes, Fadwa Louhichi, Pavlina Lucas, Simon Mahringer, Nina Mampel, Simona Marugg, Cecilia Marzullo, Edith Meier, Paul Meier, Stephan Meier, Hansruedi Meuli, Sofia Miccichè, Curdin Michael, Inger Molne, Claire Moore, Philippe Morel, Beat Müller, Nikolai Müller, Guy Muntwyler, Beate Nadler, Eibhlín Ní Chathasaigh, Humberto Nobrega, Thomas Nussbaumer, Clemens Nuyken, Stefan Oeschger, Giacomo Ortalli, Hannes Oswald, Urs Padrun, Anna Page, Suzi Pain, Pekka Pakkanen, Sebastian Pater, Gerold Perler, Giovanni Petrolito, Nicola Polli, Gabriel Pontoizeau, Ricardo Prata, Maximilian Putzmann, Carla Rada, Bettina Rageth Koch, Placidus Rageth, Jürg Ragettli, Estela Rahola Matutes, Chömbey Rawog, Benedikt Redmann, Joe Redpath, Claudia Regli, Bodil Reinhardsen, Katarina Reinhold, Nils Rostek, Annette Ruf, Brigitta Ruff, Esa Ruskeepää, Reto Ryffel, Gian Salis, Marcel Santer, Colin Schälli, Reto Schaufelbühl, Angelika Scheidegger, Enrica Schett Seglias, Christa Schmid Hartmann, Daniel Schmid, Olivia Schmid, Stephan Schmid, Martina Schoch, Serge Schoemaker, Julian von der Schulenburg, Rolf Schulthess, Emily Scott, Riccardo Signorell, Doris Sisera, Mario Sisera, Karolina Slawecka, Samuel Smith, Barbara Soldner, Astrid Sonder, Louise Souter, Annika Staudt, Thomas Steiner, Myriam Sterling, Petra Stiermayr, Melanie Stocker, Femke Stout, Kathrin Suter, Tanja Sutter, Miguela Tamo, Csaba Tarsoly, Francesca Torzo, Damir Trakic, Karin Tscholl, Florian van het Hekke, Meritxell Vaquer i Fernàndez, Maria Varela, Michele Vassella, Louise Vergnaud, Gaëlle Verrier, Katrien Vertenten, Jordi Vilardaga, Raoul Vleugels, Zeno Vogel, Urs Vogt, Burga Walli, Marietta Walli, Rainer Weitschies, Claude-Pascal Wieser, Christin Wüst, Thomas Ziegler, Caesar Zumthor, Karol Zurawski

The Work of Many

Planning and making buildings is the work of many. Inventing a large building, understanding and planning every one of its parts, taking into account the rules that underlie the art of building, the latest technology, the prevailing regulations, and finally piecing the building together out of thousands of individual parts and constructing it on site easily requires the effort of a few hundred people. As an architect, I am at once the composer and conductor of the process. I invent the work and design it. I write the architectural composition and direct its performance.

I understand my role as architect in classical terms. I determine the form of my work, I am responsible for it and, as the author, I am answerable for it. So I have the last word and I make the decisions, but not without having sought out the opinion of others repeatedly and many times over. I work in partnership, I head up the team. A good building evolves through the knowledge and skills of many. I need clients who want to create a building with me from scratch because they believe that special architectural values can thus be cultivated and that it is worthwhile following this path together. I need colleagues and specialists who plan, construct, and draw with me. I need people with whom I can talk about my designs, who criticize and praise them, who take responsibility, and who are prepared to invest their thoughts and their talent in my projects. And when we start building, the people on whose collaboration I must rely are legion: engineers, project managers, craftsmen, and specialists who manufacture the wide range of products and building parts that we need for our buildings. Without these people nothing could happen.

I love talking with a good engineer, an alert craftsman, or an experienced project manager—they are the experts and, in some cases, they understand more about constructing buildings than I do as the generalist. I love submitting my architectural ideas to them and finding common solutions to the questions raised by the project. If these discussions are successful, my design changes. It becomes concrete and acquires the distinctive contours of quality that come from actually being made.

Now, looking back on many projects and buildings, I am conscious of them again: the many people who helped me develop my ideas and implement my buildings. I thank the engineers and experts whose intelligence benefited my buildings and designs. I think with respect of the many craftsmen and construction workers who have built my buildings with great practical expertise and by the skill of their hands. I thank my partner Rainer Weitschies, who has supported me for twenty years, making sure that the quality of our designs is sustained in the process of building. I thank Hannele Grönlund. Her instinctive feel for color and the beauty of forms impresses me. I thank the people—over two hundred so far—who made and are still making contributions in my studio. All of you have helped me and are still helping me to examine and develop my design thoughts until they turn into buildings.

You are important to me.

I am deeply indebted to my wife Annalisa Zumthor. In my work and in my life.

Acknowledgments

I am happy to be able to show my projects and buildings, my design ideas
and working models in this collected edition. I cordially thank everyone involved.
I could never have done this alone.

Thomas Durisch agreed to take over the role of editor—a piece of good luck,
for Thomas Durisch knows my work and has my trust. To create this edition he
searched our archives and made a stylistically assured and atmospherically
right choice of works and images in which I recognize my way of working. He
was an integral part of the overall concept and design of the books. I thank
him most sincerely for his great contribution.

The photographers Hélène Binet, Giovanni Chiaramonte, Hans Danuser,
Ralph Feiner, Thomas Flechtner, Heinrich Helfenstein, Walter Mair,
Joël Tettamanti, and others put their pictures at my disposal. Many thanks
to them.

Rosário Gonçalves and Barbara Soldner in my studio worked with the editor
on adapting our planning materials and photographs of models for reproduction in the book; they also compiled the list of works and the bibliography.
Organizational management of the project was the responsibility of
Barbara Soldner and Olivia Schmid. I received suggestions and inspiration for
my texts from Annalisa Zumthor, Monique Zumbrunn, Thomas Durisch,
Barbara Soldner, and Olivia Schmid. Jürg Düblin, my oldest and best friend,
edited my texts with his usual patience and care. I am very grateful for
these people's work.

I thank Beat Keusch and his co-worker Angelina Köpplin for their book
design. They understood and were empathic with the world of my projects and
buildings. I am grateful to Arpaïs Du Bois for her artistic advice on the
design of my book. Her book *Where We Met* (Tielt, 2011) was an important
source of inspiration for me. We owe the outstanding quality of the reproductions
in the book to the lithographers Georg Sidler and Samuel Trutmann and
the printers at DZA Druckerei zu Altenburg. The fact that John Hargraves and
Catherine Schelbert were available to translate my texts into English, and
Yves Rosset and Catherine Dumont d'Ayot to do the same in French, pleased
me very much.

Thomas Kramer and Monique Zumbrunn of Verlag Scheidegger & Spiess
produced the five volumes with great care and professionalism.

Editor's biography: Thomas Durisch, born in Minneapolis in 1963, grew up in Binningen near Basel. 1990 degree in architecture at the Swiss Federal Institute of Technology, ETH Zurich. 1990–1994 worked at Atelier Peter Zumthor. 1995 established his own office in Zurich. Curated the exhibitions *Peter Zumthor – Bauten und Projekte 1986–2007* at Kunsthaus Bregenz (2007) and at the LX Factory Lisbon (2008); and *Architekturmodelle Peter Zumthor* at Kunsthaus Bregenz (2012–2014).

Concept: Peter Zumthor, Thomas Durisch, Beat Keusch
Design: Beat Keusch Visuelle Kommunikation, Basel – Beat Keusch, Angelina Köpplin
Artistic advice: Arpaïs Du Bois
Translation: John Hargraves
Editing: Catherine Schelbert
Proofreading: Bronwen Saunders
Image processing: Georg Sidler, Samuel Trutmann
Printing and binding: DZA Druckerei zu Altenburg GmbH, Thüringen

This book is volume 5 of *Peter Zumthor 1985–2013,* a set of five volumes which are not available separately.

© 2014 Verlag Scheidegger & Spiess AG, Zurich

New edition 2024: ISBN 978-3-03942-248-7

German edition: ISBN 978-3-03942-247-0

Verlag Scheidegger & Spiess AG
Niederdorfstrasse 54
8001 Zurich
Switzerland

Scheidegger & Spiess is being supported by the Federal Office of Culture with a general subsidy for the years 2021–2024.

All rights reserved; no part of this publication may be reproduced, stored in a retrieval system or transmitted in any form or by any means, electronic, mechanical, photocopying, recording or otherwise, without the prior written consent of the publisher.

www.scheidegger-spiess.ch

Picture Credits

Unless otherwise indicated, all sketches, plans, pictures of models, and photographs were provided by Atelier Peter Zumthor & Partner, Haldenstein.

Cordial thanks to the photographers credited below for permission to print their pictures.
In addition we thank Peter Cachola Schmal and Oliver Elser of the Deutsches Architekturmuseum DAM, Frankfurt am Main, and Richard Schlagman for their support in acquiring source material and printing rights.

© Adolf Bereuter, Dornbirn: Volume 5, p. 32
© Hélène Binet, London: Volume 1, pp. 17, 19, 20, 21, 22, 25, 32, 33, 39, 41, 42, 43, 44, 45, 46/47, 59, 60, 61, 64, 76, 77, 78, 79, 81, 84, 87, 112/113, 117, 120, 121, 122, 124, 125, 126, 127 bottom, 144, 145, 146, 147, 148, 149, 150, 153, 155, 156, 157; Volume 2, pp. 10, 11, 13, 15, 18, 20, 21, 24, 25, 27, 28, 29, 30, 31, 33, 34, 35, 36, 37, 38, 140, 141, 142, 143; Volume 3, pp. 22, 24, 26, 27, 28, 29, 32, 36, 44, 124, 125, 126, 127, 128, 129, 132; Volume 4, pp. 20 top, 122, 130, 133, 134, 135, 136, 137, 138, 139, 140, 141, 180/181, 182, 183, 184, 185, 186, 187, 189;
Volume 5, pp. 126, 128, 129, 130, 133, 134, 135
© Hélène Binet, London / Deutsches Architekturmuseum DAM, Frankfurt am Main: Volume 2, pp. 148, 149, 150, 151, 152, 153, 154, 155, 156, 157, 158, 159, 160, 161, 162, 163
© Louise Bourgeois / 2014, ProLitteris, Zurich: Volume 4, p. 170
© Polly Braden, London: Volume 5, p. 132
© Giovanni Chiaramonte, Milano: Volume 2, pp. 108, 114, 118
© Hans Danuser, Zurich: Volume 1, pp. 27, 51, 53, 55
© DMP Proces Management, Noordwijk: Volume 4, pp. 18, 19
© Christoph Engel, Karlsruhe: Volume 3, p. 130
© Damir Fabijanic, Zagreb: Volume 3, p. 25
© Ralph Feiner, Malans: Volume 2, pp. 125, 129, 130; Volume 5, p. 33
© Christian Grass, Dornbirn: Volume 5, p. 36 bottom
© Thomas Flechtner, Zurich: Volume 2, pp. 104, 105, 106/107
© Sigrid Hauser, Vienna: Volume 2, p. 26
© Jiri Havran, Oslo: Volume 4, p. 188
© Heinrich Helfenstein, Zurich: Volume 1, pp. 127 top, 128, 129
© Florian Holzherr, Gauting: Volume 5, pp. 40, 41
© Christoph Kern, Basel: Volume 1, p. 80
© Ellen Ane Krog Eggen, Oslo: Volume 4, p. 76
© Kunsthaus Bregenz, photo Markus Tretter: Volume 3, pp. 70, 81;
Volume 4, p. 28
© Peter Loewy, Frankfurt am Main: Volume 5, p. 38
© Walter Mair, Basel: Volume 2, pp. 112, 126, 127; Volume 3, p. 30;
Volume 5, p. 30
© Urszula Maj, London: Volume 5, p. 137
© 2013, Museum Associates, photo Philipp Scholz Rittermann:
Volume 5, pp. 67, 68, 72, 73, 74, 75, 76
© Garo Nalbandian, Jerusalem: Volume 4, pp. 150/151
© Natural History Museum of Los Angeles County: Volume 5, pp. 66
© Laura J. Padgett, Frankfurt am Main: Volume 3, p. 33
© Perm State Art Gallery: Volume 5, p. 141
© Rheinisches Bildarchiv, Cologne, RBA 090 006: Volume 2, p. 146 top
© Pietro Savorelli, Bagno a Ripoli: Volume 3, pp. 131, 135
© Ute Schendel, Basel: Volume 4, p. 129 top
For the work of Richard Serra: © 2014, ProLitteris, Zurich:
Volume 2, p. 150
© Shinkenchiku-sha, Tokyo, photo Shigeo Ogawa: Volume 1, p. 82
© Statens vegvesen, Norge; Nasjonale Turistveger, photo Geir Winsrygg: Volume 4, p. 79
© Statens vegvesen, Norge; Nasjonale Turistveger, photo Knut Wold:
Volume 4, p. 74
© Stiftung Topographie des Terrors, Berlin, photo Margret Nissen:
Volume 2, p. 58 top, 69 top
© Joël Tettamanti, Lausanne: Volume 4, pp. 164, 167, 168 bottom, 169

Every effort has been made to identify the holders of copyright and printing rights for all the illustrations. Should anyone have been overlooked, legitimate claims shall be compensated within the usual provisions.